TRANSCEN

A concise introduct
practice of TM – h
consciousness, the de
how to learn TM.

TRANSCENDENTAL MEDITATION

An Introduction to the Practice and Aims of TM

by

Robert Hollings

THE AQUARIAN PRESS
Wellingborough, Northamptonshire

First published 1982

British Library Cataloguing in Publication Data

Hollings, Robert
Transcendental meditation.
1. Transcendental meditation
I. Title
181'.45 BF 637.T68

ISBN 0-85030-240-4

Photoset in Wales by
Derek Doyle & Associates, Mold, Clwyd
and printed and bound in Great Britain by
Richard Clay (The Chaucer Press) Limited,
Bungay, Suffolk.

CONTENTS

CHAPTER ONE

WHAT IS TRANSCENDENTAL MEDITATION?

> I am trying to expand your consciousness, break through your macroscopic, secular set, 'turn you on', give you a faint feeling of psychedelic moment, trying to relate two sets of processes for which we have no words – speed-of-light energy-transformation process and the transcendent vision.
>
> Timothy Leary, *The Politics of Ecstasy*

There has been so much misconception about Transcendental Meditation (hereafter called TM) that probably the best way to begin a description of it is to say what it is not. Firstly, it is not, as many people imagine, a religion. It has no theological structure, and is not in any way a substitute for any of the major world faiths. A TM teacher does not ask the initiate to believe in any doctrine, or even that TM works. Indeed, they say that a certain amount of scepticism at the start generally leads to better results and that, provided it is practised correctly, the technique works by itself, in spite of any belief to the contrary on the part of the meditator. All that is needed, in fact, is enough curiosity to be willing to give it a trial. Thus, a practising Christian, for example, can take up TM without detracting from his faith. Indeed, surveys suggest that TM actually 'improves' and gives an edge to one's religious convictions just as it improves other aspects of life.

Secondly, TM is not a lifestyle, although it does by its very nature have an effect on the meditator's way of life. For instance, learning TM does not mean that one must become a member of the movement. Meditators do not dress in a certain way, or eat a certain type of food, and in fact are outwardly no different from non-meditators. Your boss may be a meditator, or the 'bus conductor, or the milkman.

Neither do meditators necessarily speak or act differently. Generally, they are less likely to become annoyed or flustered in a difficult situation and may seem more 'easy-going' than most people, though there are of course exceptions.

People who learn TM are not given direct instructions about what they should or should not do when they are not actually meditating. TM teachers do not moralize, and certainly do not claim to know all the answers to life's mysteries. For example, when questioned about 'evil spirits' at an introductory talk, one teacher replied, 'I don't know anything about them, I only know about TM.' A similar attitude is taken to the way in which a person conducts his life, even including any vices that he may have. These are left for the individual to sort out for himself. The main purpose of TM is to improve a person naturally, not to provide a set of strict rules to follow. This is an important aspect of TM and is one reason why I decided to give it a trial.

The third main point to bear in mind is that TM is not like a magic potion to use whenever things go wrong, but is a practice that should be performed at regular intervals. One does not use TM to make one 'feel better' or for the enjoyment of the experience itself, but for the long-term benefits, which occur gradually through continued practice.

This again has some relevance to one's lifestyle during the early stages. People who learn TM have different reasons for doing so. Some people feel that it may help to cure a heart condition or insomnia, while others are aware of some 'fault' in their personality which they hope to improve. We may generalize by saying that any trait which annoys one's colleagues may be regarded as undesirable, and it is this kind of trait which a person learning TM may hope to cure. However, the person may well have other 'faults' which he is not aware of, or is unable to control. Generally speaking, when a person starts to practise TM, it is the most undesirable faults which are the first to be cured. In the meantime, however, the person will continue to display other 'faults' and may even continue to enjoy activities which other people consider harmful and/or undesirable. The basic theory behind TM seems to be that continued practice will eventually lead to the meditator losing interest in all such activities, and enable him to stop simply because he himself begins to find them unpleasant. It should be mentioned, incidentally, that TM teachers are often asked to give personal advice, ranging from moral decisions to the choice of a career and domestic problems. Presumably the people who ask such questions believe that being a TM teacher automatically makes one very wise and qualified to anwer them. This is not so, and teachers have their own problems the same as anyone else. They will, however, give advice when asked, in the same way that any good friend will give advice if asked.

The important point to be made here is that learning TM will not immediately give one super-normal powers to solve problems, and an unscheduled meditation taken just because one has missed the last 'bus home or is feeling 'under the weather' may do more harm than good. Neither is a meditator necessarily a 'better' person than a non-meditator.

Extra meditations *can* be taken, under the supervision of a teacher, and these in fact are an inherent part of the weekend seminars which are provided regularly for any meditator who wishes to take advantage of them. It also seems that people who are training to become teachers have extended meditation periods as part of the course. Also, just occasionally, an unsupervised 'extra' meditation can be useful. In particular, a short meditation is good for clearing the mind prior to answering a set of examination questions. This will not help much if the subject has not been adequately studied to begin with, but it does seem to cure 'examination nerves'.

Many people feel that if TM provides the deep rest claimed, then it could be a substitute for sleep. It is not, and should not be used as such in normal circumstances. While research indicates that a daily meditation does provide as much rest as a full eight hours of sleep, there are other benefits that sleep provides, which TM does not provide and is not designed to. However, it does seem that regular practice of TM reduces any sleeping problems. Many people reported finding it easier to get out of bed in the mornings, while those who had suffered from insomnia found that TM helped them to fall asleep more easily.

Once again, however, there are exceptions to the general rule. If for some reason it is necessary to remain awake for an unusually long period, then some extra meditation can help. For example, one man had to drive several hundred miles on the continent in order to reach an important appointment. He also had to attend several meetings before setting off, which together took up most of the day, and he was due to arrive at his destination the following morning.

His original plan was to take a co-driver who would sleep during the day prior to the journey and drive at night while the executive slept in the car. However, the co-driver was unfortunately taken ill at short notice, and the executive had to drive all the way himself.

To solve the problem, the executive had his usual meditation before setting off, drove for a couple of hours, stopped for another short meditation, and continued. After another couple of hours, he stopped again and had another short meditation. He continued in this fashion until he reached his destination, by which time he was due for his normal 'morning' meditation. This man reported that although he was not quite alert as he would normally be after a night's sleep, he was able to attend the conference, and was certainly more alert than one would expect after such an ordeal.

We can summarize what has been said so far about TM by saying that it is neither an ideology nor a kind of magical process, but simply a mental technique which is added to one's normal daily activity. It is generally practised each morning and evening, for about twenty minutes each time. Outside of the meditation itself, the person conducts his life in the normal way, but should as a result of meditation begin to enjoy life more, and should gradually become better at the business of living.

Maharishi Mahesh Yogi

The founder of the TM movement, and its current leader, is Maharishi Mahesh Yogi. The names 'Maharishi' and 'Yogi' are both titles, in much the same way that 'doctor' is a title, and Mahesh is the family name. Thus it caused a great deal of amusement when an American interviewer referred to the Maharishi as 'Mr Yogi'. However, in TM circles the term 'Maharishi' is normally used in place of a name, and teachers will say such things as, 'Maharishi says ... ' and 'Maharishi's book'. While attending weekly meetings, weekend courses, etc., I also formed the habit of using this term as a name and so will continue to do so in this book. Hence, unless it is specifically stated otherwise, the word 'Maharishi' will mean this particular gentleman, and not any other Maharishi.

In a way, it could be said that Maharishi 'invented' TM, although that is a little misleading. Maharishi himself says that the technique is as old as mankind, and that all he has done is to rediscover it. TM teachers explain that he has 'simplified' or 'streamlined' the technique to make it more suited to people who live in this modern Western society which we call civilization. Whatever the truth of the matter may be, it is clear that Maharishi has at least brought the technique to the surface, and probably knows more about it than anyone else. Thus, to describe what TM is, it seems best to start with his own definition. Maharishi describes Transcendental Meditation thus:

> Transcendental Meditation is a natural technique which allows the conscious mind to experience increasingly more subtle states of thought until the source of thought, the unlimited reservoir of energy and creative intelligence, is reached. This simple practice expands the capacity of the conscious mind and a man is able to use his full potential in all fields

of thought and action.

The first point to arise from this definition is that TM is 'natural'. This means that it does not involve any kind of force or control. Unlike other forms of meditation. TM does not aim to concentrate the mind on any particular thought or to force it to follow any particular direction. This may seem strange because, to most people, the word 'meditation' conjures up a picture of a man sitting cross-legged and staring at a candle flame, contemplating a particular thought or attempting to 'make the mind a blank'. In my dictionary, the word 'meditate' is followed by the description 'to ponder, consider thoughtfully' and 'to dwell on mentally'. This again suggests some kind of control to prevent the mind from wandering. None of this applies to TM, and in fact any kind of force or control is actually counter-productive as far as TM is concerned. If the meditator follows the instructions he is given, then TM should work as described, but if any kind of control is used, the system breaks down. Indeed, Maharishi has said that if he had known what the word 'meditation' meant to Western people, he would have called the technique something else.

Note that Mahrishi uses the word 'allows', suggesting that, far from imposing any control on the mind, TM operates to remove any existing restraint. What Mahrishi is really saying here is that the mind 'wants' to go in a certain direction (i.e. towards 'more subtle states of thought') but for some reason has been unable to do so, and the suggestion is that TM removes whatever restricts the mind's freedom of action.

Of course, the word 'allows' can, in common speech, have other meanings. In an engineering textbook, for instance, the writer may describe how the removal of a certain catch or lever 'allows' another part – a piston, perhaps – to return to a state of balance or rest. In such a case, it would of course be quite wrong to consider the piston as having a will or wish to so move; it is merely being acted upon by some natural force, such as gravity. In view of this, the reader may feel that it is equally wrong to put such an interpretation on Maharishi's use of the word. Perhaps, the reader may say, Maharishi simply means that TM, while not forcing the mind, brings some similar kind of 'natural force' into play. However, during the studies I made to complete the S.C.I. course one thing that became obvious is that Maharishi is always extremely careful about using any word which may have more than one meaning. Thus, I feel sure that if he had intended something different from my interpretation, he would have used a different word. Furthermore, when we are dealing with the mind, I feel that it is right to assume that it does, or can, make such a choice without any outside influence.

I have discussed this at some length because this lack of control and removal of restrictions is such a basic part of the TM technique. Therefore without such clarification of what TM does, it is difficult, if not impossible, to explain how it works to bring about the claimed benefits. There are many forms of meditation being taught by different schools, and theoretically it is also possible that one or more schools have, without any conscious intention to usurp the reputation of the TM movement, decided to call their technique Transcendental Meditation. There is one sure method of deciding what is being taught by an organization. If the technique allows the mind to take whatever direction it may choose to take, then the school is effectively teaching a form of TM, whatever they may wish to call it. If, however, the technique does not do this, then it is not TM as described in this book. (It should be noted, however, that a 'form of TM' may not necessarily 'work' as well, or as rapidly, as the system I am describing.)

However, we see from Maharishi's definition that TM is still a 'technique', rather than a 'process', which might have been a better word if TM were an entirely natural event, or series of events. Hence, it is clear that at least something is done by the meditator to start the movement. That is, TM is not a process which can start by itself and proceed without co-operation from the person involved. At least, this does not normally occur. Some quite famous people have apparently experienced something very much like TM without any conscious decision to start. I shall have more to say about these instances later. For the moment we can say that, under normal circumstances, TM can only begin when the person in question decides to meditate and sets up the conditions which are needed to start the process. If this were not so, then we would expect 'spontaneous' meditation to be far more widespread, and, in fact it would be unlikely that there would be a need to teach it.

A further implication from Maharishi's definition is that the mind cannot free itself without the aid of the technique. Readers who have studied the works of Krishnamurti may perhaps disagree. To them I can only say that I find Krishnamurti's books fascinating, stimulating, educational and broadly enjoyable, but also incomplete. I can understand intellectually what Krishnamurti is saying, and even agree with the vast majority of the statements he makes, but I find it impossible to actually *do* what he suggests. I feel like a person who is learning to dive from a board but has become paralysed with fear. To read a book by Krishnamurti is to be instructed up the ladder and along the board as far as the very edge. One is then simply told to dive, without being told either how to do so or how to overcome the fear.

It is not my place to suggest that Krishnamurti is wrong, however. He may well be right, and incidentally I would have no hesitation in recommending that any reader who has not read any of his books should do so. In this, as in many other cases, I am forced to admit that I simply do not know. I do, however, have a point of view. I consider myself to be of at least average intelligence, and my contention is that if my inability to do what Krishnamurti suggests is due to some misunderstanding on my part, then other 'normal' people will have the same problem.

On the other hand, with TM there is no problem. In order to perform TM, it is not essential to have a clear understanding of how and why it works. One simply follows the instructions given, whereupon the system works by itself.

At this point it may be worth mentioning that the analogy I have used above was deliberate. Mahirishi has often compared TM to diving. Instead of leaving one at the edge of the board, however, starting a session of TM is like getting a push off the board, and everything that follows is a natural and direct result of the push. This explains the apparent paradox between TM being both a 'technique' and 'natural'.

The Natural Tendency of the Mind

In using the word 'natural', Maharishi is not trying to suggest that the process occurs naturally, like rain, or childbirth, or a toothache. What he does mean is that TM uses the natural tendencies of the mind to achieve the desired result. Note that this is quite different from deciding to push or persuade the mind to act as one wishes, as happens with other meditations. Given that the mind has a 'desire' to move in a certain direction, we can say that any movement in this direction is natural. Given that the mind is somehow prevented from moving in the desired direction and is unable to free itself by itself, it follows that some technique is necessary to remove the restrictions. What these restrictions are will be discussed later. For the moment, I will have to ask the reader to accept that they do exist.

However, this is only part of the story. We do not simply want to free the mind from its restrictions. The point about TM is that, like other forms of meditation, it sets out to achieve some desirable 'goal'. The difference is in the method used to achieve these aims. Other systems use control of the mind to achieve their aims, whereas TM uses the mind's desire for freedom. Hence, this freeing of the mind is a means to an end and not an end in itself.

It will be helpful here to discuss just what is meant by

the phrase 'natural tendency', particularly as regards the nature of the mind. When we talk about 'Nature' we normally mean such things as trees, animals and flowers rather than the mind, or even the kind of Nature described by the science of physics. In fact there is an important parallel between this kind of 'Nature' and the nature of the mind.

When one considers the world, it becomes clear that the one condition which occurs naturally is that nothing is ever completely still and unchanging. The earth itself moves through space. As it moves, night changes to day and spring gives way to summer. Animals (including humans), plants, trees, even mountains are constantly growing, moving, or changing in some way, however small the change may be. As you read this, you may feel that you are sitting quite still. However, although you will not notice it, your hair and fingernails are growing all the time. Rather more obviously, your heart is busy pumping the blood around your body and you are probably still digesting your last meal. Even when an animal dies, change does not cease. The skin gradually rots until just a skeleton is left, and eventually this too will rot away.

As far as 'life' is concerned, the change or movement is usually in the direction of more rather than less. Thus, animals and plants grow upwards and outwards, and this growth occurs without any conscious control. Indeed, it will continue in spite of the strongest determination to stop it. However, it can only continue so long as the right conditions exist. Without nourishment, and various other necessary factors, an animal or plant will die before its natural lifespan has ended. It is also clear that some minimum 'space' is necessary for growth, and it would appear that there is some imposed restriction on the size of any particular species.

A similar situation, according to Maharishi, applies to the mind. Its natural tendency is to grow, expand and develop as far as possible in the prevailing conditions. Within such limits, this growth and development occurs without any conscious control, but when conditions impose some restriction which cannot be overcome, then all progress in that particular direction will cease.

It will be appreciated that we can help or hinder physical growth by our own actions, within certain limits, such as by our choice of food, whether or not we take regular excercise, and so on. Clearly the same applies to the mind. Whether one's basic 'intelligence' can be altered is an interesting question, but one which I do not propose to discuss in this book. What I do wish to discuss here is the ability to obtain, store and recall useful information, and to make useful decisions about one's circumstances and surroundings, in other words the ability to 'think clearly'. This ability, whatever one chooses to call it, can be improved or expanded with the help of certain conscious actions, again within certain limits. Thus, if we take the trouble to read the newspaper and think seriously about the implications of current events, or if we study and attempt to understand a difficult text book, then we are helping to provide the right conditions for the mind to expand within. This has nothing to do with understanding everything that is read, although it is obviously necessary to have overall comprehension. An important national or international situation is normally reported over an extended period in the newspapers and a person who for some reason misses the early articles would obviously have some difficulty in understanding later ones. Even someone who has followed the whole story may not understand it sufficiently to propose a practical solution to the problem. But that is not the point. The point is that the 'thinking' or the 'attempt to understand' is what provides the right conditions for growth. Conversely, by allowing the mind to stagnate, we can restrict its growth.

It remains true, however, that the mind as a store of knowledge and experience will continue to expand in spite of any lack of effort. For instance, when something unusual or interesting occurs, one's attention is quite naturally attracted by this event, not always by a conscious choice and often in opposition to one's conscious will. Once the attention has been attracted in this way, the natural tendency is to continue to pay attention to the event in order to discover more about it. Every school teacher knows the problem of trying to hold the attention of his class when some distracting activity is going on outside.

How long the attention will be thus distracted, however, depends upon how the person feels about the event concerned, and how he feels about the other events that are going on around him. Thus, if a student is sufficiently interested in his lesson, he may glance once at the event outside, decide that it does not interest him, and return to the lesson. People who have become totally engrossed in their work have been known to go without food or sleep, or to go out in the rain and forget to take a coat, not even noticing that it is raining. Thus what needs to be stressed here is not that the mind frequently changes the object of attention, but that it will focus on whatever it finds most attractive.

In discussing this aspect of the mind, Maharishi says that it is constantly seeking greater enjoyment, and it is this which he regards as a natural tendency. The principle behind TM is that we can use the 'pleasure-seeking' tendency of the mind in order to create the conditions for it to move in the 'right' direction, i.e. towards what Maharishi calls the 'source of thought'. It is because TM uses this tendency, rather than attempting to make the mind act differently, that Maharishi regards it as natural. However, TM *is* a technique, and although it does not use force, it does give the mind what amounts to a gentle nudge in the desired direction.

The Source of Thought

It may not be clear just what the phrase 'source of thought' means. Even when Maharishi goes on to say that this is the 'unlimited reservoir of energy and creative intelligence', it does not really help very much. It is not so hard to understand that thought, energy and intelligence must have some source, but where is this 'unlimited reservoir' and what other qualities does it possess? Maharishi's answer to this question is that it is not in any specific place but exists in all places at the same time. It contains every quality that exists in the physical world and yet has no definable qualities itself It is in fact what the Christian calls 'God', what the Buddhist calls 'Nirvana', and what Maharishi himself calls 'Creative Intelligence' or simply 'The Absolute'.

Another point to arise from Maharishi's definition of TM is that the mind experiences 'increasingly more subtle states of thought'. To explain how a thought arises in the mind, Maharishi uses the analogy of a bubble rising from the bottom of the sea. It starts off very small, but grows as it gradually rises higher and higher until it 'pops' onto the surface. In a similar way, a thought starts from its most subtle level and gradually develops into what we recognize as a thought.

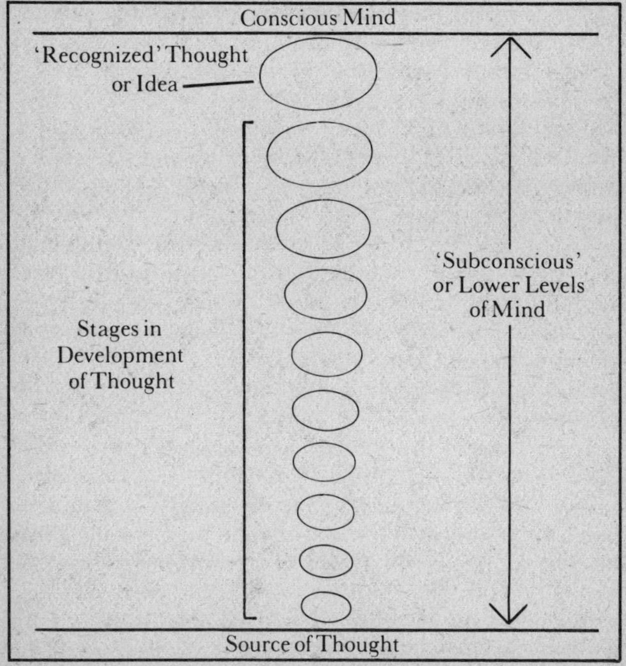

The above diagram should illustrate what I mean, and this is often used by TM teachers. The thought starts from the 'Absolute' or 'source of thought', at what may be called the borderline between this and the most subtle level of what we call the 'subconscious'. At this stage, we do not normally recognize it as a thought, but it continues to rise towards the surface of the mind.

Under normal circumstances, a thought is not recognized as such until it 'pops' into the conscious mind. During the practice of TM, however, the conscious mind is expanded and thoughts are recognized at an earlier stage of development. Moreover, regular practice of TM brings about a permanent increase in awareness, so that this early recognition of thoughts occurs during daily activity as well as during meditation itself. Ultimately, after a sufficient period of regular practise, the mind can appreciate thoughts at their most subtle level. In this way 'inspiration' and creativity are increased, and apparently the memory is also improved. This is what Maharishi means by saying that TM 'expands the capacity of the conscious mind'.

Man is not mind alone, however, and according to Maharishi's definition of TM, a man who practises it is 'able to use his full potential in *all* fields of thought and action'. Does this mean that a meditator should be better at swimming, cricket, and everything else that a man might do? Broadly speaking, the answer to this is 'yes'; but although a meditator should become 'better', he will not necessarily be 'best'. That is, a swimmer who learns to meditate will not necessarily swim better than one who does not meditate, but he should be able to improve his own performance.

It also seems that 'latent' abilities are improved, or brought to the surface. Many meditators have reported taking up various creative activities after learning to meditate, although they had not attempted such things before. Examples of these were short story writing, making Christmas cards and playing musical instruments. Some of them were able to make money from it, as in the case of a young lady who wrote an instructive article about her hobby and sold it to a magazine. One young man said that he was able to save the cost of learning to meditate by doing his own car repairs.

'Before I learned to meditate,' he said, 'I could just about change a spark plug or a road wheel and that was all. I knew how the engine worked, but was afraid to do anything in case I made a mess of it. TM gave me the confidence to try it, and because I'm also thinking clearly, I can lay all the parts out in an orderly fashion so that nothing gets lost.'

It will also be noted that Maharishi calls TM a 'simple practice'. An argument that is often raised against TM is that nothing which is easy and simple can be of lasting value. Every other technique for mental and physical development requires a great deal of effort, and most people feel that only by constantly striving to become more spiritually advanced can one reach the state known as 'Enlightenment'. Hence, we may ask just how simple TM is, and whether or not it can actually provide any lasting benefits.

The Simplicity of TM

According to Maharishi, 'All TM takes is somewhere to sit and a pair of closed eyes'. This is not strictly true, but the only other requirements are the correct mantra and the correct method of using it. Both of these are learned during a short course of instruction (three consecutive evenings) at a TM centre. Once a person has thus learned to meditate, the actual practice of it is simplicity itself. Neither is it necessary for the meditator to be of normal intelligence. Mentally sub-normal people can be and have been taught to practise TM, so long as they are able to understand the instructions given to them. To begin with, it is often necessary to repeat these instructions every day. However, in most cases, mental ability increases quite rapidly and they are then able to remember the instructions and continue without further help from the teacher.

Regarding the need for effort and control, Maharishi

feels that this view is due to a misguided understanding of what 'Enlightenment' is. We have already seen that physical and mental growth is a natural process, and Maharishi's contention is that spiritual growth should likewise be natural. The reason that it does not increase naturally, he says, is that physical stresses build up in the body and prevent the natural functions of the whole mind/body system. One purpose of TM is to dissolve and remove such stresses and this, along with the ability of TM to expand one's awareness by mental processes, is what makes it so much more effective, and simpler, than other systems.

The level of 'awareness', or spiritual development, depends not on mind alone but on the whole nervous system, and to reach an enlightened state it is necessary to improve the physical system as well as the mental processes and personality. The theory behind this will be discussed in Chapter Two, but it may be said here that normal daily life results in stresses being build up in the nervous system, and these stresses reduce the effectiveness of the system in much the same way that a blockage will restrict the flow of water through a pipe. Normal sleep will dissolve the surface stresses, and this in fact is one of the functions of sleep. Other stresses, however, become more deeply rooted and are unaffected by normal sleep processes. It is these deeply-rooted stresses that are the major cause of the 'block' to mental and spiritual development.

This fact, says Maharishi, actually explains why other systems are so difficult. While attempting to develop the mind, they use effort and control against the natural tendency of the mind. In maintaining such control, these systems in fact create more stress in the body, which hinders development rather than providing the desired results.

However, it seems that these other systems do work somehow, despite the fact that, according to Maharishi, they should not be very effective. It should be stated here that Maharishi is not actively opposed to other techniques, although some critics accuse him of this. He merely feels that since TM is quicker, and simpler, it is more useful for Western society. The aim of Maharishi's 'world plan' is not primarily to teach everyone TM, nor to set up a 'world government', but to create a race of fully developed people, and anything which helps to achieve this is, in his view, a good thing. He has in fact stated that if anyone were to approach him with a demonstrably better system than TM, he would stop teaching TM and devote all of his attention to the new system. Likewise, he feels that any system which does improve the mind and/or body, by whatever means, and whether rapidly or otherwise, must go some way towards bringing about his intended goal. However, his point is, 'Why crawl along the ground when you can get into a high-speed train?'

Although I do not propose to discuss other systems in detail, it is interesting to discover how they do work, in spite of their apparent faults. It seems that they work by a sort of round-about route, not as a result of the effort but rather in opposition to it, because the mind eventually gives up trying to achieve what is impossible.

Control of the mind is often likened to controlling a wild horse. The books state that with sufficient effort and practice, it is possible to control the mind in the same way that a wild horse may ultimately be tamed and ridden. According to Maharishi, such efforts push the mind in an unnatural direction, away from its search for enjoyment, and therefore any control which is achieved by this means can only be temporary. Unlike a horse, the mind will not succumb to any force for a long period, but will sooner or later break free. Moreover, the more that force is used, the more the mind will resist it. In effect it grows stronger because its resistance becomes a kind of 'exercise', in the same way that weight-lifting will build up a person's muscles. This makes the mind more able to overcome any obstacles to its natural growth outside of meditation, with the result that the meditator believes that his system is working. Indeed it is, but not in the manner that is intended.

In addition to this gradual growth, there may be a

sudden flash of enlightenment during a particular meditation period. It seems that what happens here is that as more and more force is applied to control the mind, it becomes like an overstretched rubber band and snaps, suddenly becoming free from any control at all. Because it has been resisting the applied force, it then shoots rapidly towards its objective with such power that it easily overcomes any obstacles in its path. By this means, the mind may reach a state of enlightenment as an opposite reaction to the original force applied.

In contrast, TM works rather like a snow plough. It not only acts in a natural direction, but also clears its own path as it moves. This will be discussed further in the next chapter.

The benefits claimed for TM will be outlined in Chapter Three, but it may be helpful to indicate here what TM means to people who help to teach it and the people who practise it.

In their book *Tranquillity Without Pills*, Jhan Robbins and David Fisher give some interesting examples of how some people feel that TM has dramatically improved their life.

A university student who had a drug problem before learning TM said that TM removed his need for drugs and helped to transform him into a good student. An alcoholic stopped drinking. A car salesman said that he learned to meditate just because 'The people connected with Transcendental Meditation are always smiling.'

Dr Robert Keith Wallace did a survey of people practising TM. In his report of the survey, published in *The American Journal of Physiology*, Dr Wallace said: 'The fact that Transcendental Meditation is easily learned and produces significant physiological changes gives it certain advantages over other ... techniques.'

In England, the system of teaching TM is organized by the Spiritual Regeneration Movement of Great Britain (S.R.M.). Their official literature states:

> Transcendental Meditation develops creative intelligence and improves clarity of perception at all

levels of experience. It is practised a few minutes each morning and evening. These sessions permit the body to gain deep rest while the mind expands in awareness. TM is unique, natural, and facilitates full development of the individual. It can be easily learned and enjoyed by just about everyone.

Although I no longer have regular contact with TM teachers, I have in the past met many of them. I can therefore state from personal experience that, contrary to what a person outside the movement may believe, TM teachers are not fanatical in their support of TM. They do not automatically agree with everything that Maharishi says. Nor do they regard the philosophy behind TM as some kind of spiritual message which must be brought to the attention of an ignorant world.

They are, in fact, a cross-section of ordinary people and not so very different from those they teach. Becoming a TM teacher is not a decision that can be made lightly. Training to become a teacher takes a long time and involves a great deal of travel, and the financial rewards of teaching are small. In fact, it can cost quite a considerable amount of money to train, particularly if lost earnings are taken into account. Broadly speaking, people who become teachers do so for reasons other than money, and the wish to 'spread the word' is only one of them. Another reason, as one teacher explained it, is that teaching TM improves one's own level of consciousness, not only because of the extra meditations undertaken, but because teaching itself has this effect.

While doing the S.C.I. course, I found that teachers often do not completely understand all of Maharishi's statements, particularly those concerning higher levels of consciousness (which I shall outline in Chapter Four), and therefore make their own interpretations. Sometimes, when Maharishi makes a statement about something not directly connected with TM, such as education, a teacher may even disagree with him. Teachers certainly have a high regard for Maharishi, but equally certainly they do not worship him or regard him as infallible.

So although the teachers may not fully comprehend the subtleties of TM philosphy, they *do* know how to meditate and how to pass on the technique to others. Although understanding the philosophy is useful for this purpose, it is not essential. It is rather like teaching someone to drive a car. You need to know what happens to the car when you press the accelerator, and you need to be able to explain this and other things to the learner, but it is not necessary to know what goes on under the bonnet.

One thing that Maharishi himself stresses is that learning TM does not mean changing one's lifestyle or rejecting the material world, as is the case with most if not all of the Eastern religions.

'We have been told,' Maharishi says, 'that we must not be material. But it is natural to be material. It is impossible not to be material. Our bodies and our senses are material. Indeed, a material basis for spiritual development is essential. We want to bring forth an inner serenity, and not a horror of the material.'

The only thing one really needs to meditate is the amount of time that it takes to do it, and although it is only two twenty-minute periods each day, this seems to be the one thing that causes some people to stop meditating. When a person learns TM, he often finds that he has more energy and wants to do more things, such as take up a new hobby. This in turn means that his life is more enjoyable, but he has less free time. Thus, he may come to feel that he can no longer spare the time for meditation.

The answer to the problem, of course, is simply one of organization and getting into the habit of meditating at the same time every day. A friend who calls may at first think it rather strange to be asked, 'Please come back later as I have to meditate.' I found that a notice outside my door saying 'Meditating, please do not disturb' became quite a joke amongst other residents. However, at least this served to let everyone know that at certain times I would not entertain them, and eventually they came to understand why. Once the habit is formed, one finds that one naturally wants to meditate when the time comes. It is, after all, a fact that however busy one may be, there are always periods when nothing of any great importance is being done. Furthermore, if one feels, as I do, that TM should be an important part of life, it becomes easier to decide to meditate rather than listen to music or watch the television. In any case, it does seem that taking the time to meditate results in a greater 'output', so that doing other things can take less time.

CHAPTER TWO

HOW DOES TM WORK?

> 'Are we nearly there?' Alice managed to pant out at last. 'Nearly there!' the Queen repeated. 'Why, we passed it ten minutes ago. Faster!'
>
> Lewis Carroll, *Through The Looking Glass*

In order to explain how TM works, Maharishi has often compared the human organism to a tree. In working to keep a tree healthy, a forester will concern himself with the whole tree. By applying nourishment to the roots he ensures that the whole tree will grow naturally. Likewise, the purpose of TM is to provide growth and rejuvenation to the whole system of mind, body and spirit. Although it works gradually, providing a little improvement each day, it works at a very deep level, at what may be called the 'root' of any defect.

When a person suffers from an illness, there are physical symptoms, but there is also a cause of the illness. Often a person may attempt to cure the illness in a way which really only treats the symptoms. A good example of this is a headache. There are many causes of headache, such as being in an environment where there is a lot of noise, or working too hard for too long, or sometimes staying in bed too long. A headache can also be a danger signal – a sign of some physical complaint. In such a case, taking an aspirin will reduce the pain, but will do nothing to cure the cause.

It is Maharishi's contention that ultimately all physical illnesses which have no obvious external cause are really due to the system itself not being entirely healthy. What this means is that although sneezing, coughing, etc., are the symptoms of a cold, and although we regard the cause as an infection, the root cause is that the system as a whole has some defect, making it less resistant to the infection. Obviously this does not apply to something like a broken leg, but even in this case a person who is fit and healthy will normally recover more rapidly than one with a 'weak' system.

Because of this, Maharishi regards treating an illness with drugs as only a temporary solution, rather like watering each dry leaf on a tree. If the leaves of a tree become dry, the forester does not solve this problem by applying water to each leaf. Instead, he applies water to the root of the tree so that the whole tree will be rejuvenated. The same applies to the human organism. If we use some method for rejuvenating the whole system, we will have fewer illnesses, and any that we do have will be cured more easily.

This does not mean that Maharishi regards normal treatment as a waste of time. If we have a headache, it makes sense to take an aspirin to relieve the pain, and if we have appendicitis it makes sense to go to a hospital for an operation. In the meantime, however, it also makes sense to do anything which is designed to improve the whole system and prevent such illnesses occurring in the first place. Apart from the benefit to oneself, there is a benefit to society. Fewer illnesses mean fewer working days lost, and fewer demands on the health service. This in turn means that those who are ill can receive better treatment.

This is not all, however. The basis of TM is that both personality and spiritual development will also suffer if the system is imperfect. Therefore any technique which 'normalizes' the whole system will also quite naturally improve these aspects of the person in the same way that it improves physical health.

Nobody in the TM movement insists that TM is essential for survival or that a person who meditates is automatically fitter than a person who does not meditate. However, Maharishi's view is that the human organism needs TM in much the same way that it needs periods of rest, good food (as opposed to a bare minimum), and exercise. That is, we can get by without it but may suffer in some way as a result.

This suffering may not be apparent to the person, since it may be a personality defect, but it will normally have some kind of visible effect, often a type of craving. For example, the person may feel a need to eat more than what is necessary for sustenance, to eat a lot of 'junk' foods, to smoke heavily, or take drugs. Most people are aware of some kind of lack in their lives, but attempt to fill this gap in different ways. Some people resort to violence for no apparent reason and others, while not exactly violent, have a tendency to become angry when things go wrong. Aggressive driving is another example. Whatever the sign, Maharishi interprets all such symptoms as the result of stress and lack of fulfilment. To state it more directly, he attributes most of the problems of individuals and society in general to the fact that knowledge of the TM technique has become lost.

Having mentioned 'fulfilment', it is worth mentioning also that the philosophy of TM does not advocate being content with 'simple pleasures', or with the prevailing conditions that one finds oneself in, as is the case with most Eastern religions. A person who takes up TM will not lose the desire to advance himself in business or to obtain desirable physical luxuries, and it is not intended that he should. Instead, the result to be hoped for is that such goals will become easier to achieve. I shall have more to say about this later.

We have seen that the natural tendency of the mind is to move towards whatever it finds most attractive, and also that there exists what Maharishi calls an 'unlimited reservoir' containing all qualities. Now, if this is the source of all things, this must include knowledge, happiness, enjoyment, and everything else that the mind seeks. It is of course true that these qualities have no physical existence. We cannot touch or see knowledge, and although we can see a person smiling, we cannot see his happiness. Nor does thought have a physical existence, and yet we experience thoughts, and must therefore say that in a sense, they exist. Hence knowledge, happiness, etc., must all have a source, and by Maharishi's definition, the common source must be this 'unlimited reservoir' to which he refers.

This being so, it is logical to assume that the source of thought and happiness would hold the maximum attraction for the mind. Thus, if what Maharishi says about the mind is true, we would expect it to go in this direction by itself, even without the aid of any technique.

In fact, Maharishi concurs with this view and often uses the argument in his own lectures. The normal mind, he says, should have direct access to the source of thought, without the aid of any technique; but the fact remains that most people do not have this ability. The explanation lies in Maharishi's definition of the 'normal' mind.

The 'Normal' Mind

It is widely accepted that the average person uses only about 10 per cent of their total mental capacity, while the remaining 90 per cent is labelled as 'the subconscious'. It would seem that a person who is regarded as a genius must use slightly more than 10 per cent, and clearly some individuals are somehow able to use more than this. This seems the most likely explanation for what are known as 'supernatural' powers, such as telepathy, clairvoyance, etc.

Personally, I dislike the word 'supernatural', since I believe that every phenomenon must be natural and explicable. By this I do not mean that telepathy does not occur or that it can be explained on the basis of what we already know about the mind. I mean that telepathy is a natural phenomenon in the same way that lightning is a phenomenon, and that as knowledge increases, it should become possible to discover the 'rules' by which it is governed. In religious terms, God never performs a miracle, but may cause things that we cannot explain, using scientific methods which we do not yet understand.

Such a state of understanding is what Maharishi regards as 'normal'. That is, he says that the 'normal' mind should be 100 per cent effective at all times. To such a mind, there is no mystery. In such a mind, what we call the subconscious has become available as a container of knowledge that can be tapped at any time. Furthermore, since such a mind has direct access to the very source of all knowledge, it is possible to immediately gain any knowledge that is lacking, just by drawing upon the reservoir.

Clearly, as far as Maharishi is concerned, the mind of the average person is not a normal mind. It is, in effect, stunted and only 10 per cent as effective as it should be. The fault, he explains, is not in the mind itself but in the condition of the whole nervous system. What prevents the mind from realizing its true potential is the large amount of stress which is built up purely by the process of living. This applies particularly to people in Western society, where we work in noisy factories, travel in the 'rush hour', and so on. Generally speaking, people in less developed societies have a slightly higher level of consciousness, not only because they are often more 'religious', but also because they have less stress. In this respect, the Indian mystic may have a point when he says that the way to enlightenment is to withdraw from the world. Clearly a person who does so has fewer stresses to get rid of and can therefore progress more rapidly. However, although this method may have its advantages, it is not suitable for people who wish to remain within a modern society. As has already been suggested, this is the main reason why Maharishi has developed a system which works regardless of the type of society one lives in.

Stress is a physical thing – an actual blockage in the nervous system which is rather like a knot tied in a water hose. Without a technique like TM, it is a block which the mind is unable to penetrate. It arises when an event in the outer world (or even just the memory of such an event) gives rise to an emotion which 'overloads' the system. Anger, terror and shock are some obvious examples of emotions that cause stress. However, any emotion may cause stress, and the difference is only one of degree. This includes the positive emotions, such as love and pleasure, as well as the negative emotions such as anger and hate.

Sudden noises, such as the ringing of the front door bell, the telephone or the alarm clock, give rise to some stress in the system, and so do any noises which the individual finds unpleasant, such as a hydraulic drill and certain types of music. When a person says that someone or something gets on his nerves, it is not always just a figure of speech.

I have said that a stress may be caused not by an actual event but by the memory of it. A good example of this is if you narrowly avoid a serious accident and then see or hear something which reminds you of this. Obviously the actual event causes stress. You step out into the road, thinking that the road is clear, or perhaps because of some personal problem you are not really thinking at all about the traffic. Suddenly you see a car hurtling straight towards you with the tyres squealing as the driver presses his foot hard on the brakes. Everything inside your body goes into double time to prepare for a flying leap, or perhaps you are rooted to the spot with fear. However, the car stops before it reaches you, and you realize that you had no need to create all this stress after all. A few days later, while sitting at home, you hear another car's tyres squealing, and this reminds you of that moment when you thought your time was up. Although there is, again, no need for it, this memory will of itself cause some tightening of the muscles, an increase in heartbeat and adrenalin, and again some more stress in the system.

Although the mind is normally regarded as having a spiritual rather than a physical nature, it clearly uses the physical brain and its associated nervous system in order to function, at least so long as we remain within a physical body. At the same time, all conscious or semi-conscious physical actions, such as tying a shoe-lace or opening a door, are controlled by the 'conscious' mind, while all that we regard as 'natural functions' (heartbeat, digestion, etc.) are controlled by the 'subconscious'. This idea is borne out by the fact that some spiritually advanced people can, apparently, stop their heartbeat deliberately. It seems, in fact, that the conclusion to be drawn from all this, and from the discussion of how the mind is expanded by TM, is that all 'mind' is really one, and the division into conscious and subconscious is only a convenience to deal with the fact that we only use 10 per cent of the mind for conscious thought. Furthermore, it seems as if 'mind' forms the bridge between the unmanifested 'source of thought' and the physical world, and that it does this by occupying a physical brain and nervous system.

This being so, it can be seen how any stresses or imperfections in the nervous system would reduce the mind's effectiveness. Wherever stresses are present in the system, that part of the system and any connections to it are effectively blocked and 'out of order', as is the case with a broken telephone line.

Clearly, however, some stresses are more permanent than others. The amount of stress resulting from the front door bell ringing is obviously less than that caused by the narrowly avoided accident, and these stresses are therefore far more easily removed. Normal sleep removes some of the stresses by giving the system a chance to relax – to 'unwind'. Other stresses, however, are caused at a much deeper level and remain in the system even after a good night's sleep. It is chiefly these deeply-rooted stresses which build up and prevent the mind from operating at its full potential. Hence, the purpose of TM is to remove these stresses and clear the path for the mind to take its natural course.

Removing the stresses, however, is not sufficient in itself. Clearly if the stresses are caused by the normal business of living, then unless we do something to change this, they will build up again almost as quickly as we remove them. Although removing them each day will help to prevent a large build-up, it will still not allow the system to be 100 per cent effective. Hence, as well as removing stresses and expanding the mind, TM has a third aspect, that of strengthening the nervous system so that is is more resistant to new stresses.

Maharishi likes to use the following series of analogies to explain how the system is strengthened. When a person does not meditate, he says, any event which can cause a stress is like scratching a line on a rock. The line represents the stress and, like a line on rock, it is difficult to remove. When meditation is started, new stresses become like a line drawn in the sand. They exist, but the next meditation should remove them in the same way that the tide will remove a line in the sand. As the nervous system is strengthened through continued practice of TM, new stresses are like a line drawn in the water. They exist only for a second and then disappear. Finally, when the meditator reaches an advanced state of consciousness, an event which would cause a stress to a less-developed system is like a line drawn in the air. As far as the nervous system is concerned, it does not even exist for an instant.

It has been stated that TM is not a substitute for sleep, and neither does the condition of a person performing TM compare with that of a person who is sleeping. There are some similarities. When meditating, the eyes are closed, and it is usual to choose a quiet environment (although this is not essential, and it is possible to meditate amidst noise and movement). TM allows the system to rest, just as sleep does. Another similarity is that there are three stages in the process – preparation, which compares to 'settling down' to sleep; the process itself; and 'coming out', which compares to waking up.

However, TM operates at a much deeper level than sleep, and a more important difference is that during TM the mind remains alert, although the body is in a deep state of rest. Research shows that the state of a person performing TM is unique to TM and does not compare with any other state such as waking, sleep, or hypnosis. TM teachers call it a state of 'restful alertness' and liken it to the state of an arrow which is drawn back in a longbow. The arrow is at rest, in that it is not actually moving; but, unlike an arrow lying on the ground, it is not an idle form of rest. Instead, the arrow is charged with the power to shoot forward once it is released.

When a person begins to meditate, he is already sitting comfortably with closed eyes, and this in itself naturally provides some rest to the system. However, if TM does what its teachers claim, the amount of rest given must obviously be much more than that gained from a quiet doze.

Extensive tests on people performing TM have been carried out by Dr Herbert Benson, who is an assistant professor at Harvard Medical School, and one of the conclusions drawn from these tests was that two twenty-minute periods of TM provide more deep rest than a full eight hours of normal sleep. In conjunction with Dr Robert Keith Wallace, Dr Benson found that oxygen consumption decreased during TM, the cardiac output decreased, and skin resistance increased. All of these are signs of deep relaxation in the subject.

In a skin resistance test, a small electric current from a constant voltage source is passed between two sensors attached to the skin. Due to perspiration, any tension or anxiety in the subject would cause the skin resistance to decrease, and this would be shown by an increase in current reading. This is the principle by which a 'lie detector' operates. During the tests, however, Dr Benson and Dr Wallace found that people doing TM gave a lower current reading than a person sitting normally relaxed.

In simple terms, it seems that TM slows down the natural processes of breathing, heartbeat and so on more than normal sleep is able to do, but without the mental states of unconsciousness or dreaming which are associated with sleep. It follows that TM is more effective at releasing stresses, particularly those stored at a deep level, where normal sleep is unable to get at them. From the work of Benson and Wallace it can be seen that the level of rest during TM is much lower than the lowest level of the 'sleep' pattern, and that the body plunges almost immediately to this deep level. The TM state is also quite different from that of hypnosis, where the metabolic rate in fact increases slightly. It should, incidentally, also be noted that although oxygen consumption is decreased, the necessary 'balance' between oxygen and carbon dioxide in the blood remains constant. That is, the decrease is not due to an unnatural deprivation, as in holding the breath during underwater swimming, for example, but is due to the fact that the system actually requires less oxygen to function.

According to Dr Demetri Kanellakos (senior research engineer at Stanford Research Institute), the human body will throw off stresses automatically when given the right conditions. When it does so, some physical motion is produced in the area of the stress, and this in turn produces a thought impulse in the brain. In other words, the release of a stress will be accompanied by a thought. Such a thought may be connected with the event which caused the stress, such as a memory of the event or a thought about something related to the event, or it may be completely unrelated to it. The process appears to be completely random, in fact. Certainly from my own experience, TM does give rise to a large number of thoughts which seem to be completely random, and each thought, or series of thoughts, is generally followed by a feeling that some stress has been released.

Sometimes, after a particularly strenuous day's work, or as a result of not having had enough sleep the previous night, a person starting a meditation will simply fall asleep. This will be a normal sleep, except that it is deeper and generally lasts for only a few minutes. This, say the teachers, should cause no concern. It is just a sign that the system needs that period of sleep, and takes advantage of the opportunity provided by settling down to meditate. Once the body has taken the amount of sleep it needs, the meditation can continue.

Generally, however, a person doing TM remains fully conscious for the whole twenty minutes, although a good part of this period may be spent in thinking a variety of unrelated thoughts, as a result of stresses being released. Moreover, the level of consciousness is actually increased by TM. This is achieved as a direct result of the release of stress, together with the mind's natural tendency to seek greater enjoyment.

What is happening in this process is that the mantra operates as the vehicle by which the mind is turned inwards, towards the source of thought. Once started, the mind continues to go in this direction by itself, simply because this is the direction which it finds most attractive. In contrast to a normal thought, which, as we have seen, starts from the source and works up to the surface, the mantra starts on the surface level and becomes more and more refined as it moves towards the source. By this means, the mind expands, which is another way of saying that consciousness is being increased.

Due to the large number of stresses in the nervous system, however, it is almost inevitable that the process will encounter some of these blockages along the way. When this happens, the combined effect of the deep rest and the quality of the mantra will dissolve the stress so that progress can continue. This removal of the stress gives rise to a thought, so that the process is temporarily stopped while thoughts are taking place. It continues when the meditator realizes that he has been thinking other thoughts and recommences thinking the mantra.

In this way, the stresses in the system are gradually reduced, so that even outside of meditation, the mind is able to operate at a deeper level than it was able to do before meditation.

An important aspect of Transcendental Meditation, and the reason for its name, is that during a meditation there is often the experience of transcending, or going beyond, the most subtle level of any thought. In other words, the very source of thought is experienced directly. Thoughts themselves cease to be experienced, which is extremely difficult to describe, since it is completely different to any normal experience. Hence it really needs to be experienced on a personal level in order to understand it, and even then a complete understanding is only present during the experience itself. When the experience is over, the mind is left with a memory of it, but being again in normal consciousness, is rather at a loss to explain or understand it. It is, I believe, what some writers call Bliss Consciousness. However, Maharishi calls it Transcendental Consciousness, and so this is the name I will use here. Although I do not wish to delve too deeply into metaphysical questions I feel that it is advisable in a book like this to at least attempt an explanation of what Transcendental Consciousness is.

Transcendental Consciousness

When one is awake (i.e. not sleeping or unconscious), one is normally aware of the tangible aspect of things. In the case of pure awareness, that is, in Transcendental Consciousness, that which is perceived is no more than one's own consciousness. In the normal waking state, one has a certain amount of self-awareness. That is, one has an underlying feeling of the self being engaged in some activity, even if that 'activity' is only lying in a state of rest. The overall feeling can be described as the thought of 'I am (walking, resting, speaking, etc....'. However, in Transcendental Consciousness, all feeling of doing and thinking has dissolved away, and there is no experience other than that which can best be described as the thought of 'I am', or 'I exist'.

The awareness of 'I' is separate from any activity. In order to simplify this discussion, and those which will follow elsewhere in the book, I propose to differentiate between the two forms by calling the 'I' of Transcendental Consciousness the 'Self' (with a capital 'S'), and the 'I' of the normal waking state will be called the 'self' (with a small 's'). Hence the term 'self-awareness' means the feeling of 'I am (engaged on some activity)', while 'Self-awareness' is the consciousness of 'I exist'.

Transcendental Consciousness does not normally last for more than a fraction of a second, but while it does so there is a profound feeling of inner contentment along with the direct realization of the Self as being separate from the normal daily experience. It is often accompanied by the realization that the Self is immortal and indestructible, which is in itself a rather overwhelming experience. People who are of a religious nature believe that the soul will continue to live after physical death. This belief is a great help towards living what may be called a good life, since it serves as a threat or warning if one is tempted, and as a promise whenever life becomes a struggle. However, there is a distinct difference between this kind of 'faith' and the direct realization which comes with Transcendental Consciousness. Similarly, it is easy to understand and agree with Descartes' conclusion that, 'I think, therefore I am'; but in Transcendental Consciousness one does not even need the evidence of having thoughts to prove one's existence. Instead, the existence of the Self becomes a direct experience.

Unfortunately, the experience does not bring that same amount of certainty into the field of normal awareness, and this is one reason why it is so difficult for anyone who has had the experience to explain it in terms that another person will understand.

As I sit here at my typewriter, I conclude that I must exist in some form, because I am conscious. However, the reason I know that I am conscious is that I can see, hear, and feel, and am thinking various thoughts. I believe that behind all this there is a Self which is immortal and indestructible. However, at the moment I am not entirely convinced of it. I recall experiencing this the last time I meditated and reached Transcendental Consciousness, and in fact this memory is the main reason that I believe it to be so. However, since I am not experiencing it at this moment, I cannot be entirely convinced through any logical discussion or intuitive feelings I may have now. I can only support the belief with the recollection that I was thoroughly convinced at the time.

Obviously, if, when I am in normal consciousness, I cannot even convince myself that Self-awareness is a valid experience, it is difficult to convince other people of its validity. However, this concept is important for any comprehensive explanation of how TM works, and even more important in a discussion of the more advanced states of consciousness, to which TM ultimately leads.

For the moment, to avoid straying too far from the purpose of the present chapter, I can only ask the reader to accept that this state can and does occur.

Consciousness does not remain in the state of Self-awareness for the reason that the nervous system will still have stresses remaining. Transcendental Consciousness cannot become permanent until the last stress has been removed, at which point it becomes Cosmic Consciousness, and is present even during normal activity. What has happened when it does occur is that the mind has somehow found a path through the stresses and so has reached the source of thought in spite of the fact that some blockages remain. Maharishi calls this 'tiptoeing through a herd of elephants', and this is a very good illustration of what happens. Thus, immediately after the experience, the mind comes back to the process of meditating, having thoughts, and so on. There may be several 'dives' into Transcendental Consciousness during a meditation, but some may be so brief that the meditator does not afterwards have any recollection of the experience.

As fascinating and pleasant as Transcendental Consciousness may be, it is not the purpose of TM to experience this for its own sake. Rather, the experience is just another step on the path towards Cosmic Consciousness, or the state which Maharishi regards as 'normal', when there are no stresses and the mind is operating at its full potential.

An anaology often used by TM teachers is that of drawing water from a well. To take water, we do not just drop the bucket into the well, letting it stay there for ever. Instead, we lower the bucket into the water until it is full and then bring it up again. Similarly, it is not the 'dive' of TM by itself which brings about Cosmic Consciousness, but regular practice of TM alternating with normal daily activity. Each experience of the state of Transcendental Consciousness will leave an effect in the mind. Each session of TM dissolves a few more stresses and brings a slight increase in the depth of consciousness. However, if one were to remain in

Transcendental Consciousness, or remain meditating, all the time, there would be very little benefit from these improvements. The increase in the level of consciousness would be of no practical benefit. By resuming normal daily activity after meditation, the successive daily gains are strengthened and built up to a useful level. By doing this one is, in effect, taking part of the Absolute and storing it up in one's own consciousness. It is by this regular alternation of TM and activity that the mind is expanded at the same time that stresses are released.

The Practice of TM

This seems to be an appropriate point to describe what doing TM actually involves. The first essential is to be relaxed and comfortable, and because of this there is no set posture to be adopted. However, it is better to be sitting upright, if possible. The back should be straight and the head held up, at least when the meditation starts. During meditation, the head may drop forward or lean to one side, and one should not use any conscious effort to prevent this, but when the realization comes that this has happened, then one should gently raise the head to an erect position again.

A person who is ill or disabled can meditate lying in bed, and, generally speaking, the more meditation that can be done during illness, the better it will be for recovery. However, it is not a good idea for a normally fit person to take the morning meditation while still in bed, since there is then a greater tendency just to fall asleep again. It is better to get up, wash and dress, and generally spend a few minutes getting oneself into the 'fully awake' state. For some people this will take longer than others. Personally, if I do not meditate, as happens sometimes if I get up late and do not have time, I find that I am not entirely 'awake' until after the first tea break, but I have always had this problem and I regard it as something which will presumably be cured at some time as 'purification' of the system progresses. When it does happen I usually take an extended tea break and find somewhere to meditate at work.

As regards food, it is better to eat after meditation than before. However, if you wake up feeling very hungry then this feeling could spoil the meditation more than the business of digesting the food, so in that case it would be better to eat something. In the event, a light breakfast such as cereal and a boiled egg will not make much difference. However, it should be remembered that the whole metabolism is slowed down during TM, and that this includes the digestive processes, so that meditating soon after a large meal can cause some discomfort.

Some people who have done other forms of meditation before may wish to adopt the lotus position for TM. There is nothing wrong with this idea, but conversely there is no reason to adopt the posture if it is in any way uncomfortable. In other words it makes no difference and is simply a matter of personal choice. The same thing applies to the position of the arms and legs. Some people like to sit with the arms along the line of the legs, while others prefer to 'cup' the hands together in the lap. Again, some people keep their legs at a ninety-degree angle, while some people stretch their legs out with angles crossed.. There is no set recommendation other than what the individual finds most comfortable.

In TM, probably the most important principle is to be comfortable. Thus, if we start meditating in one position and find that this becomes uncomfortable, there is nothing wrong with easing gently into another position during the meditation. Likewise if we feel a sudden urge to scratch the nose, sneeze, cough or whatever, we do not repress it or try to ignore it. We can also open one eye slightly to glance at the watch or clock to see how the time is passing, i.e. whether the recommended twenty minutes has been completed. Conversely, however, one should not give way to such urges too easily so that one is continually scratching, twitching and so on, because once the meditation gets going, the mind becomes filled with thoughts, or with the mantra, and the condition of the body is forgotten for the most part. In most cases, having a number of urges to move about or twitch is a sign that a large number of 'big' stresses are being released, and this gives rise to the physical movement or sensation as well as a thought impulse.

It is best not to start meditating immediately, but to sit quietly for about half a minute as if one is preparing to take an afternoon nap. Just sit quietly with the eyes closed, make yourself comfortable, and relax. Do not think of anything in particular, but just allow whatever thoughts come into your head to be experienced and then pass away naturally. It would be incorrect to use this time to consider any problems that have cropped up during the day, but at the same time it is incorrect to consciously avoid thinking about problems. In other words, we do not make a decision to think about this or that, but just experience whatever happens.

It is possible to meditate almost anywhere, even amidst distracting noises. I have myself meditated on a bus, on a train, in a noisy public house, on a park bench with a pneumatic drill working nearby, in a room where the television was on, and in an underground station, and in every case I still obtained some benefit from the meditation. However, as far as possible, it is best to turn off any distracting noises and arrange that one is not disturbed for about half an hour. If you only occupy a part of the premises and are used to having people call on you at odd times, make up a little card to hang outside the door to tell people that you do not wish to be disturbed, or to simply say 'back in half an hour', from which they will naturally assume that you have gone out. In company, it is still possible to meditate at the usual time by using a little imagination, even if the company is such that the word 'meditate' may cause a raised eyebrow. One can invent other reasons to leave the room or close the eyes for a short while, such as a headache or 'I forgot to feed the cat'. If you remain in the room, they will probably think that you have fallen asleep, and there is normally no problem in letting them continue to think so. Of course if your friends can understand that you wish to meditate and why, so much the better. In other cases, I have found that the best solution is to let them make whatever jokes and comments may amuse them, and just treat the whole thing very lightly. There is no sense in rejecting TM on the basis that your friends would not understand it; nor is there any sense in falling out with a friend just because he finds it strange or amusing.

One thing that is definitely not a good idea is to set the alarm clock to ring at the end of the twenty minutes, or to set a clock/radio in the same way. There is very little worse than having a sudden loud noise near the end of a meditation, when it is often at its deepest point, and if one finds that it is generally difficult to estimate the time, it is better to glance at the clock or watch at intervals during the meditation. In any case it is not crucial to stop after the recommended twenty minutes, so long as one does not deliberately extend the period. I have on occasion commenced a meditation, immediately sunk very deeply into it, and then glanced at the clock to discover that thirty minutes have passed without my being conscious of time passing, although I was not actually asleep.

For the same reason, it is best to take the telephone receiver off the hook. If, despite all possible precautions, somebody does call during your meditation and nobody else is in, then the recommended procedure is to stop meditating, take a minute or so to readjust, and then answer the door. Then, if possible, tell the caller politely that you are in the middle of something important, and ask that they come back later. When the caller has gone, then commence meditating again for the rest of the twenty minutes, allowing for the time of the interruption. This can be a nuisance, but it is better than letting the person ring the bell endlessly, and also it is more polite to them if they know you are in. Obviously, if the reason for the call is something that will only take a few seconds (such as paying for the milk) it is better to do this immediately rather than tell them to come back.

Using the Mantra

During the initial course of instruction for TM, one is given a mantra, and this same mantra must be used on each occasion. (However for long-term meditators there is an 'advanced technique' using a different mantra). After about half a minute of sitting quietly with the eyes closed, the mantra will normally come into the mind without any conscious effort. It almost seems that the mind delivers the mantra for the purpose. That is, after a series of the normal kinds of thoughts that one would expect while sitting quietly, the mantra will come along just like any other thought. When this happens, the meditation can begin.

If for some reason the mantra does not appear, one should make no effort to think of it or remember it. For example, I sometimes find that I have a sort of mental block in trying to recall the name of a person whom I want to talk about, and although I know the name is somewhere in my memory store, it just will not come out. When this happens I often think of the letters of the alphabet to see if I can recall what letter the name starts with. It always comes to mind eventually, but to do anything like this to start the mantra is quite contrary to the purpose of TM, which is to allow things to happen naturally. In fact, it is very unlikely that the mantra will be forgotten, and indeed it can sometimes enter the mind when you do not really want it to. Even after a break in my practise of about six months, I found that on my first meditation the mantra came to mind almost immediately. Hence, if it does not come right away, it is best to just continue thinking idly until it does appear.

During the meditation, the mantra is held in the mind and repeated silently, in preference to any other thought. However, the vital point about TM is that no effort is used to keep the mantra in mind if it tends to slip away. It is a little difficult to describe just what this means, and it may be clearer to the reader if I describe what *not* to do.

In the book *Who Am I? – A Book Of World Religions* by Martin Ballard, the first stage of the Hindu yoga excercises is described thus:

> *Concentration*. It is first necessary to clear the mind of all those flitting images which normally occupy it by pinning it down to a single object. The nature of the object itself does not matter; it is only important that it should fill the mind to the exclusion of everything else.

I can think of no better description of what *not* to do in TM. It does not matter if the mantra tends to slip away and is replaced by other thoughts. Indeed, it is a sign that the mantra is doing its work in relaxing the system and giving the mind the opportunity to move towards the source of thought. The mantra may also change in some way, even to the extent of seeming to be a completely different sound, and this again is a good sign. However, it is still necessary to keep the mantra 'in mind', very gently, at whatever level it exists. Sometimes it will be near the surface level of the mind and hence will be quite a strong thought. At other times it will be at a deep level, when it will seem to be a barely discernible 'ripple' in the mind, existing along with other thoughts. Sometimes it will 'transcend' or be at such a deep level that, as far as your conscious awareness is concerned, it has disappeared altogether.

At intervals during meditation, the meditator will experience what seem to be normal thoughts, and mostly quite random thoughts which have no direct relationship with the meditation. These may range in type from a very ordinary and simple thought, such as a decision to have kippers for tea, up to some deeply philosophical thought such as the existence and nature of God. Beginners, and sometimes long-term meditators, may even think that the meditation is a waste of time. All such thoughts, of whatever type, are simply an indication that some stress is being released in the system. Hence, the meditator should not concern himself with the *meaning* of any thought, but simply realize that he has been thinking and then return to the mantra. In particular, the thought that the meditation is boring or a waste of time does not mean that the meditation is not working, or that it is being done incorrectly. Probably it means quite the reverse, i.e. that some particularly deep stress is being released. This stress, for instance, may have been caused by some deep depression of frustration in one's life. However, quite often the nature of the thought has nothing at all to do with the original cause of the stress.

Unlike other forms of meditation, a person doing TM does not regret the presence of other thoughts, even if these thoughts and the mantra appear to be in the mind at the same time. Neither should any effort be made to replace thoughts with the mantra. At the same time, however, one should not go on thinking other thoughts in order to follow an idea to its logical conclusion, or because the thought concerns a pleasant subject. This may be explained better by quoting Maharishi's instructions, as taken from a set of checking notes:

> In this meditation, we do not concentrate, we do not try to think the mantra clearly. Mental repetition is not a clear pronunciation, it is just a faint idea. We don't try to make a rhythm of the mantra. We don't try to control thoughts. We do not wish that thoughts should not come. If a thought comes, we do not try to push it out. We don't feel sorry about it. When a thought comes, the mind is completely absorbed in the thought. When we become aware that we are not thinking the mantra, then we quietly come back to the mantra. Very easily we think the mantra and if at any moment we feel that we are forgetting it, we should not try to persist in repeating it or try to keep on remembering it. Only very easily we start and take it as it comes, and do not hold the mantra if it tends to slip away.

Maharishi also offers the following advice about what to do if the mantra and other thoughts appear to exist in the mind simultaneously:

> There is no need to try to stop thinking because thoughts are a part of meditation. Even if the mind is

> filled with other thoughts, while the mantra is going on, there is no conflict. Our concern is with the mantra and if other thoughts are there along with it, we do not mind them and we don't try to remove them. We are not concerned with them. We innocently favour the mantra.

Later in the notes, he offers the following analogy as an example:

> If [a thought] comes along we don't mind. Neither we try to maintain [the thought] with the mantra, nor do we try to forget about it. Mantra is all our concern. Innocently we favour the mantra as when we are walking along a road, if someone is found walking by our side, we just don't mind.

The actual frequency of thoughts depends to a large extent on the state of the nervous system when meditation begins. If there is a lot of surface stress, perhaps due to a particularly busy day at work, an awkward customer, etc., then the meditator may complete the twenty minutes with the feeling that he has been thinking randomly for the whole period, and not meditated at all. In fact, however, such a meditation is more beneficial than one in which the mantra remains on the surface of the mind and thoughts are few and far between.

A similar rule applies if the meditator has frequent urges to glance at his watch to see how much time has passed, or has such thoughts as, 'This is silly', or, 'I'm tired of sitting here doing nothing'. Sometimes the twenty minutes seem to pass by in a flash, and at other times it seems to be a very long time indeed. Generally, the longer it seems and the more boring it feels, the greater the amount of stress released. This is not a statement put out by the TM movement to 'trick' people into believing that TM works. The meditator can test it for himself at the end of the meditation. After a 'long' and 'boring' meditation, he should feel less tired and in a better mood than before the meditation, and the difference between the two states should be greater than it is after a 'short' meditation. The amount of stress released will be similar, but those stresses released in a 'short' meditation will have been at a deeper level, so that the person may not feel such a great difference when they are released. Hence, short of some emergency situation occurring, the twenty minutes should always be completed regardless of any thoughts about stopping halfway through.

After the Meditation

At the end of the twenty minutes, the meditator stops thinking the mantra and continues to sit quietly with closed eyes for about two or three minutes in order to become readjusted to normal experience. This gives the mind the opportunity to return to the 'surface' level of thinking slowly and naturally, and is therefore very important. If the meditation is broken off suddenly, there may be a shock to the system and the meditator may get a headache – rather like a diver suffering from 'the bends' after surfacing too quickly

This is of course particularly important if the meditation has been very deep, and in this case the meditator may well feel rather reluctant to open his eyes anyway. If this happens, or if the meditator feels a little 'groggy', then a longer period can be taken, and in general the longer the better. However, even if it is felt that the meditation has not been very deep, it may have been deeper than one imagines, and the period of sitting quietly should always be at least two minutes.

It is also advisable to open the eyes slowly and to look down at the floor, away from any light source or bright colours, so that the eyes have a good chance to readjust. It should be remembered that the optic nerve has been inactive for the most part during the meditation, and suddenly opening the eyes to look at a brightly-coloured picture may cause what amounts to an overload. This will of course be small and temporary, but is precisely what meditation seeks to avoid.

Within a minute or so after opening the eyes, the meditator will be 'back to normal' and can then stand up and resume normal activity. Most meditators seem to find, however, that the first few minutes after a meditation are the most pleasant period of all. They feel more relaxed and yet more energetic, less concerned about any upsetting event that has occurred during the day, and more willing to carry out any tasks that need to be done next. They often seem to see things more clearly, as if they are noticing them for the first time, or seeing them in a slightly different way. Colours often seem brighter (hence the above warning) and perception in general seems to be enhanced. Although such feelings begin to fade as one resumes normal activity, they do not entirely disappear, and meditators find that whatever needs to be done after meditation becomes easier to do and more enjoyable.

Now that the method of performing TM has been briefly outlined, my own advice is *not* to attempt this alone. This is not a comprehensive manual. In the long term, it is easier and much more beneficial to have individual tuition from a qualified TM teacher. In giving this advice, I would like to remind the reader that I am no longer connected with the TM movement in any way, and so have nothing to gain by making this recommendation, but genuinely believe that it is the best course of action for anyone who wishes to start TM. For those who wish to ignore this advice, I should like to add one further caution. In almost every form of meditation, the sound 'Om' or 'Aum' is recommended as a mantra. If you wish to adopt these forms of meditation instead of TM, then by all means use this mantra, but to use it with the TM method can result in quite a dramatic change in the personality.

'How To Learn TM' is the subject of the last chapter. As I have said in my introduction, I do not feel that it is my place to either recommend or otherwise that the reader should learn TM, but the chapter is there for those who do decide to learn. Most readers, however, will probably have quite a number of questions left so far unanswered. One of these may be: 'Why, if TM is so simple, is it necessary to teach it at all? Instead of setting-up a world-wide network of teaching centres and charging fees, why doesn't the Maharishi just write a book telling everyone how to meditate?'

When one completely understands how TM works it becomes clear that TM simply cannot be taught by the written word; nor is it possible to teach people correctly in groups. Being so simple, there is a tendency for the written word to be misunderstood, and any set series of instructions given to a group is really no better than a book in this respect. The difference between following Maharishi's instruction to 'innocently favour the mantra' and concentrating on the mantra is a very subtle one. Hence, any person reading my instructions and following them blindly could easily be concentrating on the mantra without realizing that he is doing so. This is particularly likely if some other form of meditation has been tried in the past. Such concentration actually prevents the mantra from doing its work, and so it is absolutely vital to the success of TM to avoid this.

On the first evening of instruction, the initiate is told how to meditate and is then left by himself to follow the instructions. Following this, he is asked to answer a set of simple questions by means of a form. These questions concern the initiate's experiences during the first meditation, and how he feels as a result of it, and from the answers given the trained teacher is able to deduce whether the initiate has understood and followed the instructions, or whether he has been doing something wrong. In the latter case, the teacher will know what instructions to give to clarify the method, and can continue to give additional instructions until it is clear that the initiate is meditating in the correct manner. It also seems that different people have widely differing experiences following their initial instruction, sometimes even before they are left to try a 'solo' meditation. The mere fact of knowing one's mantra can apparently have quite a startling effect. In such cases, it will require the full attention of the teacher to deal with the situation.

One other reason for individual tuition is that in order to meditate, one must have a mantra. TM teachers absolutely refuse to reveal how a person's mantra is chosen, and they recommend that one should not reveal one's own mantra to anyone else. This has naturally led to some criticism, with the suggestion that the mystery is solely for the purpose of maintaining the 'individual tuition' method, again for financial reasons. At least one critic has argued that there is probably only one mantra, and that the recommendation is made so that meditators will not compare mantras and so discover the fraud.

As regards the last suggestion, there is very little evidence one way or the other, but what I have been able to gather suggests that this theory is untrue. I could not find anyone willing to reveal their own mantra to me. However, one married couple said that they had told each other their mantras, and that these were different. I believe that the mystery *is* to protect the 'individual tuition' method, but for valid reasons. What the actual number of mantras may be can only be a guess. The reason given for not revealing one's mantra is simply that it is designed to go deep into the mind and not come out through the mouth. One interesting point is that teachers insist that the method of choosing the mantra is quite mechanical, according to some predetermined system, and has nothing to do with the teacher's personal 'feeling' about the initiate.

So, what are the 'valid reasons' for the mystery? From discussions with the teachers, and my own deductions I have reached the following conclusions:

1. Individual instruction is necessary, not for financial gain but for the reasons I have already given.
2. This being so, it would be unfortunate it untrained people started to teach it to their friends, since their friends may then start doing it incorrectly and the untrained meditator would not know how to correct the fault.

3. The friend, continuing to perform TM incorrectly, would not gain any benefit from the technique, and would naturally assume that it does not work as claimed. Thus, not only would he stop meditating, but would then be quite unwilling to learn the technique properly.
4. This result is not only bad for the meditator's friend, but also bad for anyone whom the friend talks to about it, and ultimately bad for the movement's overall aims.
5. The movement cannot prevent meditators from telling their friends how to meditate, and so the only logical safeguard is to withold information on how to choose a mantra for them.
6. It is mainly due to incorrect teaching that the knowledge of the technique became lost through previous generations. By keeping the full knowledge within a strictly organized structure, it can be kept intact for a much longer period. This in turn is good for Maharishi's 'World Plan'.

CHAPTER THREE

THE GOALS OF TM

> When suffering grows, the invincible force of nature moves to set man's vision right and establish a way of life which will again fulfull the high purpose of his existence.
>
> Maharishi Mahesh Yogi

Within the TM movement, and also by some other interested parties, the theory behind the operation of Transcendental Meditation is regarded as a science. It is called the Science of Creative Intelligence, normally shortened to 'S.C.I.' Transcendental Meditation is held to be the practical application of S.C.I., in the same way that finding the height of a distant object is the practical application of the science of Trigonometry. S.C.I. attempts to explain just how and why TM works.

In simple terms, the scientific method consists of observing a phenomenon, constructing a theory to explain what happens, and testing this theory. The first theory is often no more than a guess, but the theory will be modified if it does not completely satisfy the test and ultimately, if the tests are sufficiently rigorous, the final theory can be regarded as an undeniable fact of life.

Not every reader will regard this as a good thing. One of the reasons for the growing interest in Eastern philosophy, the occult, etc., is that this is a reaction against increasing materialism, and especially against modern technology. Many people feel that scientists often ignore any test results which contradict their pet theory, or simply pronounce that a certain event is impossible without really testing it at all. Examples of such events are psychokinesis, the 'physical' appearance of ghosts, and the objective existence of UFOs.

In most cases, however, the scientific method is valid,

and without it many of the obvious advantages of modern civilization would not exist. With S.C.I., as with other sciences, two consecutive events are observed, and the assumption is made that event 'B' is directly caused by event 'A'. From this, it can be predicted that event 'A' will always be followed by event 'B'. There is then an attempt to isolate event 'A' from any other events which may have caused event 'B' to occur. If this is done successfully, and event 'B' still follows event 'A' every time, in all circumstances, we can safely say that the theory has been proved, at least until we discover some exception to the rule. Even under laboratory conditions, it is not always possible to rule out other causes, but the closer we can get to this ideal, the more exact the science will be. Ancient rites, customs and 'old wives tales' are the opposite of this. The advice that 'an apple a day keeps the doctor away' may be good advice, but it is unlikely to be scientifically accurate, for even if it is found that no one who eats an apple every day has ever had to visit a doctor, there may well be other good reasons for their good health. It is only when such other possibilities have been ruled out that a theory can be called a scientific law.

One theory connected with TM is particularly interesting. Although it has not yet been conclusively tested, it has received some support from the scientific community, and is known as the '1 per cent rule'.

After a number of investigations into how his overall plan was progressing, Maharishi felt that a definite pattern was emerging. This pattern can be summed up by the theory that if only 1 per cent of a given community is regularly performing TM, then the whole community will experience some benefit. Glossop, in Derbyshire, is such a place. In Glossop, just over 1 per cent of the residents are practising meditators. Perhaps it is only a coincidence, but Glossop has a significantly lower crime rate than any comparable community anywhere in England. Moreover, scientists have recently discovered that the '1 per cent rule' seems to apply throughout nature. For example, if 1 per cent of the atoms in a piece of metal are magnetized, then the whole unit will become magnetized in the same direction.

The benefits claimed for TM on a personal level have also been the subject of extensive scientific tests, and in general the results of these tests have supported the claims. Among these are increased learning ability and academic performance, relief from insomnia, reduced use of alcohol, tobacco and non-prescribed drugs, decreased anxiety, decreased blood pressure, improved resistance to disease, improved job performance, and improved relations with other people. For those who are interested, a whole series of test results is available from the Spiritual Regeneration Movement.

Anything which can improve a large number of individuals will ultimately have effects on a global level, and with this in mind we will examine Maharishi's World Plan.

Maharishi's World Plan

The objectives of Maharishi's World Plan are as follows:

1. To develop the full potential of the individual
2. To improve government achievements
3. To realize the highest ideal of education
4. To eliminate the age-old problems of crime and all behaviour that brings unhapiness to the family of man
5. To maximize the intelligent use of the environment
6. To bring fulfillment to the economic aspirations of individuals and society
7. To achieve the spiritual goals of mankind in this generation.

Although the plan is so far-reaching as to seem almost impossible, a proper understanding of the TM philosophy shows how these aims can be regarded as being realistic and attainable. It will be useful, therefore, to examine them one by one in more detail.

Goal 1 – To develop the full potential of the individual

We have already seen what Maharishi means by 'full potential of the individual', and in general terms we have discussed how this may be developed through the use of the TM technique. However, it will be useful to restate the points made and enlarge upon them here, so that the reader can more easily understand how this goal relates to the others.

It is, in my view, the most important of the seven goals. Not because the individual is necessarily more important than society, but because a society can only exist as a collection of individuals. Hence, anything that effects a large number of individuals will have a similar effect on the society as a whole. The reverse is not always true, however. For example, better schools will not necessarily result in an overall improvement in the level of education; better roads will not necessarily reduce the number of road accidents.

TM, in particular, is designed to operate at an individual level. Hence, if it cannot improve the individual, it is not likely to have any great effect in bringing about the other six aims of the World Plan.

Even a limited study of life's many mysteries shows that, in general, a normal person uses only a small part of his full potential. (I am using 'normal' here in the accepted sense, not in Maharishi's definition.) As far as mental capacity is concerned, it is generally accepted that we use about 10 per cent of the mind's total capacity in order to carry out our daily lives, and even when solving a difficult problem we do not use a great deal more than this. Yet, by using this small percentage of our capacity, we have developed a workable economic system and made great advances in science and technology.

It is true that our economic and political systems are not perfect, and that our technology has created problems as well as solving them. However, considering such restricted use of mental capacity, it is hardly surprising that we have so far failed to create a perfect world, and indeed it is quite astonishing that we have made as much progress as we have. Clearly if it is possible to develop the ability to use the remaining 90 per cent of our mental capacity, then even greater advances can be made. Telepathy and clairvoyance are only two examples of what may become 'normal' abilities. At any rate, it should become easier for any individual to achieve his own ambitions.

In improving the individual, we should not restrict ourselves to only one kind of ability. Rather than merely improving mental ability, it is necessary to also improve temperament and physical health. Even in a normally fit person, there is some room for improvement on a physical level. We may feel that we are using our full capacity for physical work when doing something strenuous, particularly if this is followed by a feeling of exhaustion. Because we feel 'worn out' after the effort, we may conclude that we could not have done any better. However, the point about improving one's physical resources is that it should then be possible to do more, or to do the same amount without feeling tired. Some people may feel that they already work quite hard enough to earn a living, and that the idea of doing more is not very appealing. However, even if the worker is not paid according to output, there are still distinct advantages in becoming more productive. A business which enjoys the benefits of efficiency is more likely to be in a position to give pay rises and to provide more amenities for its staff. Generally speaking, greater output means cheaper goods, and even if businesses are reluctant to reduce prices, this effect should at least postpone any increases.

There are more direct personal benefits, too. Less tiredness after a day's work means more enjoyment can be derived from one's leisure hours; and if we can become more efficient at leisure activities we shall have more time for other things.

Eastern philosophy views desire as the main cause of man's problems. It is said that suffering is due to the fact that we desire things we cannot obtain. It is said that this leads not only to frustration and jealousy, but may also lead to crime.

There can be little doubt that desire does lead to suffering and crime, and no doubt reducing desire would also reduce the effects. However, there is clearly a limit to what is possible in this respect, and it also seems to me that reducing desire is not always a good thing. As regards what is possible, there is no way that we can seriously expect people to give up a desire for food, clothing and housing. There are also things that are by no means essential to life (such as television sets, washing machines, and so on) but which many people in Western society regard as necessities.

The ideal of abolishing desire may be a commendable spiritual goal, but it is impossible for most of us to follow. I do not consider myself a complete materialist and certainly would not advocate material prosperity at the expense of spiritual growth; but as Maharishi says, 'It is impossible not to be material'. Even a saint must eat and clothe himself.

In Maharishi's view, the cause of all suffering is not desire itself, but the *inability to fulfil one's desires*. This in turn results from the inability to make full use of one's mental and physical capacity. The robber steals not because he wants to steal but because he is unable to satisfy his desires through legal activities. Given the ability to maintain a well-paid job (and 'ability' here includes all the necessary personality characteristics), he would cease to steal and become a useful member of society. Likewise, people who cause suffering to others in order to fulfil their desires should be able to find other ways of achieving their aims. If such people can be made more aware of the suffering they have caused, and develop a more 'Christian' attitude, it may well be that they will then start using their wealth to help others who are in need. Instead of wasting money on unnecessary luxuries, the money could go to aid the poor, or to improve the Health Service, or to reduce unemployment by opening new businesses. In short, the solution to suffering is not to eliminate desire, but to improve the individual and to make it easier for desires to be fulfilled.

This is the purpose of Maharishi's first goal, and it is worth restating that the wish to 'develop the full potential of the individual' includes all of an individual's characteristics – emotional and spiritual as well as mental and physical. Hence, if one of our desires is to become a better person, or a better Christian, or to achieve spiritual perfection, Maharishi intends that this goal also should become attainable. His belief that we can develop such abilities is based on the following argument:

Progress and evolution are the nature of life, as we have seen in the first chapter. It is equally natural for an individual to desire better health, greater happiness, greater knowledge and greater achievement. Considering that growth is natural, it is very strange that life is a struggle. The fact that life *is* a struggle suggests that some natural element is missing, and that it is this lack which is preventing normal progress.

This element is Creative Intelligence. Because we lack the ability to draw upon the reservoir of Creative Intelligence, we also lack the ability to operate at full potential, at full efficiency.

This ability will be restored if we can directly experience the source of Creative Intelligence and open a channel through which we can draw upon it during daily life.

Transcendental Meditation provides the direct experience of the source of Creative Intelligence by expanding the mind, and opens the channel by refining the nervous system.

We have seen in Chapter Two that the human organism can be compared to a tree. If a tree is suffering from some lack of moisture, this fact will be made evident by the visible sign of dry leaves. Likewise, lack of the ability to use full potential is shown by suffering and crime. The kind of action which is normally taken to improve an individual (such as punishing a criminal and treating a health disorder with drugs) is like applying moisture only to the dry leaves. TM is like applying moisture to the root of the tree, where it is most beneficial. Just as watering the root benefits the whole tree, so TM improves all aspects of the individual.

Goal 2 – To improve governmental achievements

In general terms, problems like a high rate of inflation and a high level of unemployment are now regarded as the responsibility of the government. An individual will, by his actions, have some effect on such problems, but it is mainly government policy which either cures the problems or makes them worse.

Maharishi believes that no government is evil by design, although some individuals may misuse their position to gain wealth and power for themselves. He also feels that every nation's leader has aspired to do more for his people, at least at the outset of his career, but for a variety of reasons has been unable to fulfil his ambitions.

Some of the reasons include a lack of foresight, poor advice from ministers, lack of support from trade unions, and the actions of other nations. Each of these conditions will present some problems to the leader and restrict his course of action.

This kind of difficulty is often overlooked when it comes to assessing any particular government's performance. Despite the fact that a prime minister or president is a human being, and his ministers too are human beings, it would seem that some critics expect them to perform superhuman tasks and to somehow overcome all the difficulties, including those over which they have no control. When a recession in another country reduces that country's demand for British goods, for instance, when the raw materials which we must import increase in price, and when production is constantly hit by strikes, absenteeism, etc., the government is still expected to ensure that Britain has a favourable trade balance.

It should be noted that Maharishi's second goal is to *improve* governmental achievements rather than to create a state of perfection. It may ultimately be possible to create a 'heaven on earth', or it may not; but in the meantime any improvement that can be made must be regarded as a step in the right direction.

The way to improvement is to increase the efficiency of the nation's leader, the cabinet ministers, and everyone down to the humblest worker, and also to improve relationships at all levels of society.

As may be expected, Maharishi believes that this can be brought about through the practice of TM. On a governmental level, by adopting TM the nation's leader and ministers will be able to use their full potential in finding solutions to problems. On a managerial level, TM can bring both greater efficiency and greater creativity, which would help businesses to expand even in difficult times. Workers too should become more efficient, which will naturally lead to an improvement in their condition.

There should also be an improvement in co-operation at all levels, between workers and management, between management and government, and indeed between any two groups which have conflicting aims.

Goal 3 – To realize the highest ideal of education

According to the pamphlet 'Education in Britain', published by Her Majesty's Stationery Office, 'The aim of the State system of education in Britain is to provide a comprehensive service for all who can profit from it: to secure for children a happier childhood and a better start in life; to ensure a fuller measure of educational opportunity for young people and to provide means for all of developing the various talents with which they are endowed and so enriching the inheritance of the country whose citizens they are'.

According to Maharishi, the ideal of education is 'To create a fully developed man who is knowledgeable, resourceful, responsible, successful, fulfilled, and of maximum use to himself and to others. Thus, an educated man is not merely one who has knowledge, but one who is able to use that knowledge effectively.'

Although these two statements are phrased very

differently, both of them are basically saying the same thing. That is, that education is intended to provide a means whereby a man can become a fully developed and useful member of society, and can also achieve personal satisfaction.

The ability to gain knowledge depends on the level of consciousness. According to the Science of Creative Intelligence, a man who has Unity Consciousness is able to obtain knowledge directly from the Absolute. This claim will be examined in the next chapter, but for the moment we will consider only the more usual means of gaining knowledge.

A man who is normally awake gains knowledge through the senses. That is, by observation, touch, taste, smell and hearing. The knowledge may come directly through these senses or from a book or teacher, or it may require some experiment and intellectual analysis. For most practical purposes, the knowledge thus gained by a normally alert person will be complete, correct and useful.

On the other hand, a man who is drunk or drugged is less able to perceive what is real, and his intellectual activity is confused. Hence, the knowledge gained by such a man is less useful, and may be incorrect. Similarly, if one of the five senses are made inoperative, by a blindfold for example, the knowledge gained from using the other four senses may be incomplete and incorrect. Further, the knowledge gained by a man who is dreaming is an illusion, while a man who is sleeping or is unconscious gains no knowledge at all.

Thus, improving the level of consciousness also improves the ability to gain useful knowledge. We have seen that TM is designed to improve the level of consciousness and expand the mind, thus making the 'container of knowledge' larger. Hence, it should also improve the ability to gain knowledge, and to retain it for practical use.

However, TM does not stop there. Besides improving the ability to gain knowledge, it is also designed to improve the personality characteristics of the student.

This includes such things as attention to the subject, willingness to study, memory etc., as well as creativity, health, and the ability to co-operate with others.

Part of the World Plan, as an adjunct to teaching TM itself, is to set up a network of colleges under the general authority of Maharishi International University, and some progress has already been made in this direction. In an M.I.U. course, the students will study the Science of Creative Intelligence along with the kind of subjects which other universities cater for.

One advantage of this system is that the 'entrance requirements' place much less emphasis on examination results and are more concerned with the student's suitability for the course he has chosen. The general view seems to be that if the person has an inherent ability to be a good lawyer, doctor, or whatever, he should not be held back by examination failure. With the help of TM, and through the M.I.U. course, he should be able to reach a useful standard of knowledge about this subject.

Another important advantage is that in an M.I.U. course, the subjects are not kept in compartments. For instance, although a law student may cover such subjects as commercial law, legal history, and the structure of the courts, he will also discover how these subjects relate to each other, and to other subjects which may not be included in a normal university course. This will enable him to make better judgements in any given situation. Generally speaking, a man who is able to draw upon a wide range of knowledge is more successful in his career than one who is restricted to knowledge which falls within the sometimes narrow boundaries of a university degree curriculum.

Only a few M.I.U. colleges are operating at present, and all students have to bear the cost of their course themselves. Maharishi hopes that it will ultimately be possible to obtain a government grant for an M.I.U. course and for an M.I.U. 'pass' certificate to be accepted as at least equal to an ordinary degree.

Goal 4 – To eliminate crime and all behaviour that brings unhappiness

The thought that TM can improve one's efficiency leads to an interesting and rather amusing speculation. If, as is claimed, TM can help a swimmer or a businessman to be more successful in their activities, then perhaps it can also help a criminal to become a more successful criminal!

Maharishi, however, assures us that this would not happen. We have seen that the reason for crime is an inability to succeed by legal means, and it is this which TM is designed to improve. Thus a criminal who learns TM should gradually come to realize that his actions are harmful to himself and others, and will find other ways of satisfying his desires. In fact there has already been some progress towards teaching TM to prisoners, and the results have been generally successful, with released prisoners being less likely to commit further crimes.

By similar reasoning, we can see that there should be a similar reduction in other activities that cause unhappiness, such as violence and heavy drinking, as people become more successful and suffer less from the frustrations which lead to such activities.

Goal 5 – To maximize the intelligent use of the environment

There is currently a great deal of concern about the fact that technology seems to be advancing at the expense of the environment. Apart from the problems of pollution and shortage of natural resources, there is a threat to the very existence of some animal species. In addition, many areas which are of historic interest or are tourist attractions are being gradually destroyed, except where specific regulations are made to preserve them.

In Maharishi's view, such conditions are a result of a lack of creative ability on the part of industrialists, businessmen and city planners. Given this creative ability, he says, such people will not only achieve their aims without destroying the environment, but will also find ways to restore and protect it, and to use natural resources with the utmost efficiency. Where factories, offices and living accommodation are planned, a more creative architect will be able to design them to look beautiful as well as serving a practical purpose. It is possible to design buildings to blend in with the environment rather than standing out against it, and in this way we can preserve or even improve the environment instead of destroying it.

Goal 6 – To bring fulfilment to the economic aspirations of individuals and society

Most people's economic aspirations can be summed up as having an income sufficient to cover the cost of necessities, the luxuries which they wish to enjoy, expenses such as holidays, and a reasonable level of savings.

For society as a whole, the economic aims are broadly similar to those of the individual. But again, in spite of the fact that the aims are reasonable, there is a severe shortage of funds at both the national and regional level. Maharishi believes that the same solution applies to both individual and social problems. As an individual becomes more creative and begins to use more and more of his potential, he will become more able to obtain the level of income he needs, and will also find more efficient ways of using it. For example, a man who is unemployed due to some character defect will become a more reliable person and should then be able to obtain and keep a good job. A man who is unemployed due to economic conditions will be able to learn a new skill, or perhaps devise a scheme for earning his own livelihood.

Likewise, as individuals in a society become more creative and efficient, the cost of a given project should be reduced, so that more projects can be undertaken with the same amount of funds. Also, if those who make the economic decisions are more efficient, they will make better choices and there will be less waste of resources.

Goal 7 – To achieve the spiritual goals of mankind in this generation

By their very nature, the spiritual goals of a person or of mankind in general are difficult to classify. However, perhaps they can be summed up as the desire to comprehend ultimate reality and to develop the kind of abilities which, as yet, scientists refuse to acknowledge or only dimly understand. Such abilities include, for example, mental telepathy, clairvoyance, telekinesis, and levitation. Also among the spiritual goals, we may include the desire for world peace and greater equality and happiness.

Many people today are talking about some drastic change in society, which they believe is due to occur within this generation. Some people believe that we are on the verge of the biblical Armageddon, with a nuclear war followed by a new, more religious, society. Others refer to it as the New Age, or the Age of Aquarius.

Maharishi believes that such feelings are due to the progressive workings of Creative Intelligence, which people are somehow aware of, but cannot quite fully comprehend. Creative Intelligence, the ultimate 'power' behind life and the physical universe, is also the means by which everything grows towards its most developed state. This being so, Creative Intelligence is always working towards improving what may be called the conditions of life. It is, however, a form of evolution and is dependent upon the existing conditions. When mankind is at a low spiritual level, when humans are not making sufficient attempt to improve themselves, then Creative Intelligence is more restricted.

Throughout history, different religious leaders have attempted to bring about a perfect society, but all have so far failed to accomplish this goal. Maharishi believes that their success was only partial because their knowledge was incomplete. What has been missing, he says, is the ability to experience and consciously tap the source of all power and intelligence. Now that this ability has once again become available, we have a situation in which mankind and Creative Intelligence can work together, towards the same aim. In this situation, achievement of spiritual goals should become easier. With the gradual spread of TM, the overall level of consciousness in society has already been improved, and this explains why there is an underlying awareness of change and improvement.

These, then, are the seven goals of Maharishi's World Plan. It will be seen that achievement of these goals is based on the assumption that TM develops creativity, the ability to gain and use knowledge, efficiency, personality, health, and the overall level of consciousness.

Although some aspects of TM are incapable of being proved except by personal experience, the tests that have been carried out by various independent authorities do seem to support the majority of its claims. These tests may be classified according to the six categories which I have outlined, as follows:

1 – Creativity

'Increased creativity' was found to result from TM according to tests carried out by Dr Demetri Kanellakos of the Stanford Research Institute. These tests compared meditators with non-meditators and also compared the level of creativity achieved by each meditator before and after learning TM. It was found that creativity increased after learning TM, and it was also found that the average level of creativity among meditators was higher than the average for the group of non-meditators.

2 – Ability to learn and use knowledge

Studies carried out at the University of Hawaii indicate that the average grades of students who practise TM are significantly increased, and continue to increase as long as regular practice of TM is maintained. Other studies indicate that TM results in the integration and co-ordination of different areas of the brain, leading to more orderly thinking. When a person is performing TM, E.E.G. signals from the two hemispheres of the brain fall into phase with one another. This is a situation which is unknown amongst non-meditators.

3 – Efficiency

As well as increased creativity, Dr Kanellakos found in

his studies that meditating subjects have 'increased energy and efficiency ... productivity ... and concentration'. Studies made by other researchers showed that meditators display an increased motor response to a stimulus. For example, they take a significantly shorter time to push a button in response to a light.

4 – Personality

Studies carried out by Dr David Orme-Johnson at the University of Texas showed that meditators are 'less irritable and jittery' than non-meditators. At the University of Cincinnati, thirty-five students were given psychological tests. Fifteen of these students were then initiated into TM and the whole group was re-tested two months later. The meditators significantly increased their scores in 'self-actualization' tests, while the non-meditators remained the same as in the first test.

5 – Health

Dr Robert Keith Wallace of the Harvard Medical School conducted a number of studies, finding amongst other things that TM reduces physical and mental tension. He feels that TM can help to control blood pressure and also aids recovery from disease and injury. Dr Wallace conducted a survey to test this theory and found that 67 per cent of the subjects reported significant improvements in their physical health. Benefits reported included lower blood pressure, fewer colds, fewer headaches and weight loss.

Although it is not directly related to health, the abuse of drugs, tobacco and alcohol probably has an adverse effect on the user's general health. It is now generally accepted that smoking at least contributes towards lung cancer and heart disease. Many smokers would themselves admit this, and yet for most smokers the need to continue is greater than the fear of the result.

A similar situation applies to alcohol and drugs. To begin with, the user may feel that he can keep his consumption within reasonable bounds. However, the difference between sustained heavy drinking and being an alcoholic is a very narrow one, and with many unprescribed drugs it takes an even shorter time to become 'hooked'.

There have been a number of studies of TM in relation to drug abuse, and the general result of these shows that after learning TM, the vast majority of drug users cease using these drugs. Figures quoted by the University of California, for example, were 84 per cent in the case of marijuana, 86 per cent with hallucinogens, and 86 per cent with hard drugs like cocaine. That is, 86 per cent of former addicts ceased using addictive drugs.

Similarly, Dr Herbert Benson reported after his survey that meditating subjects 'decreased their use of hard alcoholic beverages and smoking. The magnitude of these changes increased with the length of time the subject practised Transcendental Meditation.'

6 – Level of Consciousness

As far as I am aware, it is not yet possible to directly test an advanced state of consciousness scientifically. We cannot connect a person's brain to a machine which will indicate when he is in Transcendental Consciousness, or Cosmic Consciousness.

However, it is possible to test for more normal states of consciousness, i.e. deep sleep, dreaming and the waking state. It is well known that the dreaming state is shown by rapid eye movements, while E.E.G. readings will show whether a person is awake or asleep.

During studies on meditators, it was found that they spontaneously produce theta waves in the brain, and this condition is believed to indicate a deep state of tranquillity.

As an indication that TM does increase the level of consciousness, the only other instance in which theta waves are known to occur spontaneously is in meditating Zen monks. It is worth adding that this result is only found in monks who have practised the meditation for many years, while in TM practitioners it is found quite a short time after initiation.

During the preparation for this book, I personally conducted a survey amongst meditators in order to obtain their opinions about TM. The subjects were chosen entirely at random and included subjects of various ages and from various walks of life. The length of time that the subjects had been practising TM ranged from one month to four years. No actual tests were carried out, but subjects were simply asked to answer such questions as, 'Do you find TM enjoyable?'; 'Does practising TM make any difference to your way of life?'; 'What benefits, if any, have you experienced from TM?'; and 'Would you recommend TM to your friends and relatives?'

It was expected that the reports would be generally favourable, but the number of favourable reports, and the enthusiasm with which they were given, came as a surprise. Almost all subjects stated that meditation was enjoyable and gave benefits including better health, more energy, better memory, less anxiety and tension, and a general improvement in the level of contentment. Likewise, almost all subjects stated that they not only would recommend TM to their friends, but had already done so. In many cases, these friends had noticed the improvement and had thus been persuaded to learn TM themselves. (Interestingly enough, in these cases it frequently occurred that the meditator himself did not notice the changes which his friend had noticed.)

The most surprising result that was obtained from this survey was that very few people would say anything at all against TM except for the fact that it was sometimes a problem to find time to do it. Not that all reports were favourable. A few meditators complained of getting headaches after meditation, while some felt that nothing conclusive had resulted from their adopting TM. Some subjects reported that they had temporarily stopped meditating for one reason or another, but most of these still considered it beneficial and intended to start again. The number of adverse reports, however, was very small and only came about after a deliberate effort to find complaints.

CHAPTER FOUR

THE SEVEN STATES OF CONSCIOUSNESS

> Pay attention, incorrigible optimist, sister to the monk, romantic tired girl, open your eyes, and open your ears. Get ready because here it comes. Ushered in with a sob, there are words. There is a sentence. It comes on the wind and it crashes through the time barrier and it says, 'You are indestructible.'
>
> 'Daybreak' by Joan Baez

Most people only experience three different states of consciousness – namely deep sleep, dreaming sleep, and the normal waking state. As regards deep sleep, it is not really true to say that a person experiences this state at all. It is, however, a state which occurs naturally, and it is obviously very different from either of the other two states. It can therefore be considered a third state of consciousness, despite the fact that it is really *un*consciousness. The different characteristics of the three states can be summarized as follows.

In the deep sleep state, consciousness is absent. The sleeper is not only unaware of events in the outer world, but also his self-awareness is absent. Since nothing is experienced during this state, there is no memory of the state when the sleeper comes out of it.

In the dreaming state, there is a certain amount of self-awareness and some awareness of the outer world. However, both of these experiences are illusory. When a person is dreaming, a sound in the room or in the road outside may be 'heard', in a sense, so that the sound gives some direction to the content of the dream. The resulting dream experience, however, is not the same as the experience that would result from hearing the sound in the waking state.

Much of the content of a dream involves activities that

would be considered either impossible or highly unlikely in the waking state. For instance, we may fly through the air in dreams, or meet some person that in real life we can only admire from a distance. The awareness of the self is also largely illusory in the dreaming state.

In the waking state, there is both awareness of the self and awareness of the outer world. It is true that not everything we experience during the waking state is real, since appearances are often deceptive. However, ignoring deep philosophical arguments about what is and is not 'real', it can at least be assumed that one's experience during the waking state is far more reliable than the experience of dreams. This applies both to self-awareness and the awareness of the outer world.

There are other states that may be experienced by an individual, such as drunkenness, being drugged, being hypnotized, and so on. However, the general characteristics of all such states compare to one or other of the three 'natural' states already described. That is, one is either unaware, experiencing an illusion, or having an experience which can broadly be defined as 'normal'.

According to Maharishi, however, there are in all *seven* distinct states of consciousness, each with its own characteristics. The first three states are of course those described above. Maharishi's terms for the remaining four states are 'Transcendental Consciousness', 'Cosmic Consciousness', 'God Consciousness', and 'Unity Consciousness'. In order that the reader may have a better understanding of the difference between these states and the other three, I shall attempt to describe them. To do so, however, I can only re-state what Maharishi has himself said about them and add my own interpretation of his statements.

Transcendental Consciousness

In daily life, we have a kind of dual awareness. There is the awareness of the outer world, but at the same time there is the awareness of the self as distinct from the other people and objects in the world. It is not a complete separation, however, for we are only aware of the self through the senses, and the thoughts that we have about our surroundings. The self is perceived to be performing actions, or being acted upon. Examples of such impressions are, 'I am chopping wood' (which is performing an action on the material world) and 'I feel a cold wind' (which is being acted upon by a material event).

Transcendental Consciousness arises when, during the course of a meditation, the mind transcends all thought and feeling and experiences 'pure awareness'. As we have seen in Chapter Two, this gives rise to the experience of a different kind of awareness of oneself, which I am calling 'Self-awareness'. In this state, consciousness of the Self is present without the awareness of any relationship between the Self and the outer world. Indeed, the outer world is not experienced at all in this state, and even thought itself comes to an end. Hence, Transcendental Consciousness bears no relation to normal waking consciousness. One is conscious of one's own existence, but nothing else.

This facet of TM is probably the most difficult to explain and consequently the most misunderstood. It seems logical to assume that in order to be conscious, one must be conscious of something external, some sensation, or some thought. If there is no sound, no feeling, no smell, no taste, no vision and no thoughts, what is there left to experience? Without any experience, how can one be said to be conscious? Have we not already seen, in the discussion of deep sleep, that lack of any experience indicates unconsciousness?

The answer is that what remains is the Self, and it is this which we become conscious of. This is not the self that has been experienced during daily life, but the inner Self. In daily life, the ordinary person is never aware of the Self at all.

In daily life, we use the word 'I' quite frequently, without ever considering just what this 'I' really is. We see, we feel, we have likes and dislikes, and we have thoughts and opinions. In general, we seem to believe that the 'I' is made up of all these things and cannot exist without them. However, if it is possible to cut off all sense impressions and all memories, to forget about likes and dislikes, forget about opinions, and finally stop all thought, then what is left is the entity which has been engaged on all this activity. We cannot experience the Self directly in normal circumstances, because it is behind the wall which it has been busily constructing around itself, a wall of sensations, ideas, and beliefs. This does not mean, however, that it is impossible to experience it at all, and the fact that we cannot describe it does not mean that it cannot exist.

We can, in fact, go some way towards describing it. We can, for instance, say that it is 'unbounded' or 'infinite'. We can say that Self-awareness is the experience of the Self as unchanging and eternal. The problem is that in order to describe something, we have to use words, and all words have a finite range of meaning. Words like 'infinite' are not really descriptive words at all, but only a vague attempt to explain something which is completely beyond normal experience. The existence of pure awareness cannot be proved by logical argument, but only by personal experience. However, we can give some argument for its existence by contrasting it with the deep sleep state.

If pure awareness does exist, there is really no reason to believe that it is ever completely absent. Its very nature would seem to indicate that it is present in everyone at all times, just as thoughts are always present during the normal waking state. However, as we have seen in the discussion of stress as it relates to consciousness, the normal mind does not have the clarity of perception needed to experience pure awareness. Thus, when we go into a deep sleep, pure awareness does not take over in place of normal awareness. During TM, however, the mind *is* made clearer, and so when all other experiences are removed, the mind can experience pure awareness, if only for a split second.

In certain circumstances, it is possible to experience this state even when the person is not practising TM. This has apparently happened to several famous people.

Alfred Lord Tennyson described to a friend how he experienced a state which he could not describe, but which he called 'boundless being'. Tennyson apparently had this experience several times, and he seems to have adopted a form of TM which brought it about. What Tennyson did was to repeat his own name silently in his mind, which means in effect that he was using his own name as a mantra.

H. Warner Allen, the writer, had a similar experience, and described this as 'drawing strength from a limitless sea of power'. Others such as Newton, Einstein and Fermi have given broadly similar descriptions of the moment when they had the experience of creative insight which led to their discoveries. In these cases, it seems that the experience was spontaneous, presumably when the scientists were physically relaxed but mentally alert, thinking about the problem and just letting ideas float around in their heads. Although this condition is not quite TM, it would be very similar and so may easily lead to a spontaneous 'dive' into a state of Transcendental Consciousness.

Cosmic Consciousness

The fifth state of consciousness, Cosmic Consciousness, is the main goal of TM as far as the average meditator is concerned, although it is not the ultimate goal. According to the Science of Creative Intelligence, each meditation brings Cosmic Consciousness (C.C.) a little closer. Cosmic Consciousness is the state in which Self-awareness (Transcendental Consciousness) is always present along with the waking, dreaming, and deep sleep states.

Although Transcendental Consciousness is a pleasant and interesting experience, it is of no practical benefit by itself. It is rather like a chest of treasure lying on the ocean floor, where a diver can examine it but can do nothing practical with it. Its only real value, during meditation, is that it gradually comes to be experienced outside of meditation, and ultimately becomes a permanent experience. It is this permanent experience of

Transcendental Consciousness which Maharishi calls Cosmic Consciousness.

This occurs when the nervous system has been completely cleared of all its stresses, so that the Self can shine through unclouded. Maharishi has compared this process to cleaning a mirror. When a mirror is covered with dust and smears, it is only able to give a poor reflection, but the cleaner the mirror is, the clearer the reflection will be.

In C.C., the 'I' is perceived to be completely separate from any thought or action by the self, and from any other material event. Furthermore, it remains unaffected by any outer event and any condition of the mind and body. A man who is in Cosmic Consciousness will still experience thoughts, sensations, etc., but always the Self remains behind all this, unchanging and unaffected. One of the most interesting concepts about this state is that for the first time one can experience and enjoy deep sleep!

A person in C.C. acts very differently to a person in normal consciousness. He enjoys a state of permanent contentment whatever his physical condition and whatever events are going on in the world around him. This is not to say that he will lose interest in material things. Indeed, S.C.I. shows that he will gain even more enjoyment from material possessions and from his relationships with other people. He will also continue to strive to make his surroundings and relationships more appealing. Unlike a normal person, however, he will not feel a need to use people and things for his own gratification, but will automatically be more generous and helpful to others. Hence, with more people in Cosmic Consciousness, life as a whole would be much better.

Once Cosmic Consciousness has been achieved, progression to the next two states is automatic and apparently quite rapid, at least compared to the progression from the normal state to C.C. In fact, it often happens that a person will have brief experiences of these higher states even before C.C. is fully established.

God Consciousness

The sixth state is what Maharishi calls God Consciousness. For the benefit of any agnostic or atheist readers, I should point out that in choosing this title, Maharishi is not attempting to make a declaration that God exists. Certainly he is not investing God with a personality in the way that a Christian understands the term. However, to understand God Consciousness, it is necessary to accept that the physical world, like the human form, has both a 'body' and a 'spirit', or what Maharishi refers to as 'manifest' and 'unmanifest'. When we think about such a spirit, it is normal to refer to this as God, whether or not we believe in the existence of a personal God. That is, we can consider God as the unmanifest spirit and the physical world as God's 'body'. It could equally be called Creative Intelligence, which has a less personal implication. However, the term 'Creative Intelligence Consciousness' is a clumsy phrase and does not seem quite so useful as a description of what God Consciousness is.

We have seen that in Cosmic Consciousness, there is the permanent experience of the inner Self. Likewise, in God Consciousness, there is awareness of the unmanifest 'spirit' underlying the physical world. A rock is not just a rock, but is the physical manifestation of creation by the Absolute Reality (which we can call God or Creative Intelligence). It is not too hard to understand this concept on an intellectual level, whether or not one believes in a personal God. We know that all physical objects are made up of atoms, and that atoms in turn are made up of smaller particles. We also know that all atoms display qualities of motion, electrical charge and attraction. From this, we can form a concept of some unseen force that gives all these atoms the qualities that we have discovered. As in the case of the Self, the fact that we do not quite understand this force does not mean that it cannot exist. The important point about God Consciousness is that the ultimate nature of the physical world is directly experienced, and not just intellectually understood.

Unity Consciousness

The seventh state is Unity Consciousness. As would be expected, this state is the most difficult to understand, and I can only give an indication of what this state involves. In fact, Maharishi has only revealed this state to TM teachers within the last few years. Thus, apart from the few who have devoted a lot of time to the study of philosophy and metaphysics, even the teachers find it difficult to give a good explanation of what Unity Consciousness is.

Broadly speaking, Unity Consciousness means what its name suggests – the awareness that all is one. All aspects of the creation, including the Self and the 'spirit' of the world, are perceived to be manifestations of a single ultimate reality, that which Maharishi calls the Absolute. Thus, the Self is no different from the unmanifest form of other people and other objects in the world. Everything we see, everything we feel, and everything we think or experience, is merely the one ultimate reality at work. To quote the Eastern doctrine, 'I am That, thou art That, all this is That.'

One may think from this that when Unity Consciousness is achieved, the Self merely dissolves away and the individual either ceases to exist (as an individual) or else we are back where we started, in a normal state of consciousness. After all, in normal life we feel related to people and objects in the world. We feel that we are part of the world and that our experience of the world is part of us. It would seem that when Unity Consciousness is achieved, we merely obtain proof of what we have suspected all along, so why bother to achieve it?

This argument, however, misses the point. Unity Consciousness is not the awareness of being part of the physical world, but the awareness that 'spirit' is the basis of all things, including the Self. Moreover, in normal life we are *not* closely attuned to people and events, although we may feel that we are. If we have a good friend, we may feel that we know that person well enough to predict how we will act in a given set of circumstances. However, most people only reveal that which they want us to know. The friend may have many thoughts and opinions which for some reason he has not revealed, and it is possible that when placed in the circumstances we imagine, he will act quite differently to the way we expect.

It seems that when a man reaches the state of Unity Consciousness, he still somehow retains the awareness of the Self as being separate and unaffected by any material event, and the Self still retains a certain amount of individuality. Maharishi explains this by using the analogy of a wave on the ocean. A wave is part of the ocean, and in the same way the Self is part of the Absolute. Both the ocean and the wave are made of the same substance, and in the same way the Self and the Absolute are all one 'spirit'. Even so, the wave can be thought of as being distinct from the ocean, a separate entity due to its form and motion. In the same way, Maharishi says, the Self of a man in Unity Consciousness retains its individuality and awareness.

However, because a man in Unity Consciousness has, in a sense, 'merged' with the Absolute, knowledge in any form can be obtained instantly, directly from the source of all knowledge. This does not mean that a man in Unity Consciousness knows everything, but what it does seem to mean is that he is able to obtain the answer to any question, merely by thinking about it.*

* Readers who wish to know more about the subject of this chapter and consciousness in general are recommended to read *Seven States of Consciousness* by Anthony Campbell (Gollancz, 1973).

CHAPTER FIVE

AN OUTLINE OF THE TM MOVEMENT

> There is a higher ordering and we all are nothing else than its agents.
>
> Adolf Hitler, 9 April 1938

The Maharishi's understanding of TM came to him from his teacher, Swami Brahmananda Sarasvati. For the last thirteen years of his life, Swami Brahmananda was Shankaracharya of the Jyotir Math monastery, in the Himalayas, and before that he was a strict recluse. He is known among members of the TM movement by the much simpler name of 'Guru Dev', and so I shall henceforth use this name to refer to him.

The story goes that the young Mahesh was looking for a teacher, met Guru Dev, and decided to become his disciple, despite the fact the rest of the Mahesh family were bitterly opposed to the idea. Apparently it came to the point that Guru Dev had to visit the Mahesh family and inform them that, since their son refused to return to them whatever they said, they might as well release him to the Guru Dev's care. Eventually, the family agreed to this and made no further attempts to persuade their son to return. Maharishi in fact became Guru Dev's favourite disciple, and it is doubtful that he ever saw his parents again.

When an Indian decides to study under a mystic, he takes what amounts to a new start in life, and has nothing more to do with what has gone before. At any rate Maharishi has little to say about this period of his life, except that he was drawn to Guru Dev 'like an iron filing to a magnet'. He followed the mystic like a shadow, and when Guru Dev died, Maharishi had no clear idea of what to do next. He spent a long time as a recluse, just meditating alone in a cave in the Himalayas. After a time, he was occasionally joined by another man.

'We hardly ever spoke,' says Maharishi. 'After all, there was really nothing to talk about.' A good indication of their mood is the story that Maharishi relates, of an occasion when the other man came into the cave with his hair completely shaved off. When Maharishi asked why he had shaved it, the man replied, that it was simply one more material thing to worry about, and it was better to get rid of it.

One day, while meditating, Maharishi had the thought that he should go to a certain village in India. He had no idea why he should go there, and at first he just ignored it. However, the thought persisted, and eventually he decided to mention it to his companion. Apparently, this same thought kept coming to Maharishi over quite a long period. The first time that he mentioned it, the other replied that it was just a meaningless thought, and it would pass. However, it did not pass, and although Maharishi hesitated to bring it up again, he eventually did so. When this had occured several times, the companion eventually said that Maharishi had better go to this village, and then he would see that there was nothing there and could come back to meditate in peace. 'This is holy ground,' his companion said. 'All the rest is just mud.'

Maharishi made his way to the village. He was of course quite penniless, but that did not matter because it was considered an honour to have a holy man in the house, and he soon found free accommodation. He still had no idea what he was supposed to do in the village, and merely wandered around for a few days until he began to feel that his companion must be right. However, before he finally decided to leave, he was approached in the street and asked if he gave lectures. Although the idea had not occured to him, Maharishi felt that this would be a good idea, so when the stranger said that he could hire a hall, Maharishi agreed to speak. He spent all of the next day deciding what to speak about.

It was at this meeting that the TM movement really started, for while giving his lecture, Maharishi suddenly decided that it was time to 'spiritually regenerate the whole world', and made this announcement in the middle of his speech.

Not surprisingly, he received a thunderous applause, and the meeting hall filled to overcrowding as people gathered round to see what was happening.

'Why didn't you tell us this before?' the organizers wanted to know. 'We could have hired a bigger place.'

'I didn't know,' Maharishi replied. 'I've only just thought of it.'

A short time after the lecture, however, Maharishi realized that although his basic idea might be a good one, it was beset with problems. 'I suddenly realized,' he says, 'that if I was going to go around the world teaching everyone myself, it would take several generations to complete the job!'

To solve this problem, Maharishi decided to set up a network of training centres, and to simplify TM so that other people could be trained to teach it, without having to reach the state of Cosmic Consciousness themselves. His plan is to have 1000 such centres, and for each main centre to train 1000 teachers. This will give one million teachers, and if each of these teaches 1000 people, then at least a large percentage of the world's population will learn the technique.

This, then, is the way that the TM movement is organized. As yet, of course, the plan is only 'in progress', but the number of existing centres is by no means insignificant. The movement has in fact come quite a long way since the four young men collectively known as the Beatles went to see Maharishi and caused TM to hit the headlines. There are national centres in Britain, the U.S.A., Canada, Australia, New Zealand, South Africa and India, each governing a network of smaller centres throughout each country. In addition to this, there are trained teachers in Argentina, Austria, Brazil, Denmark, France, West Germany, Greece, Holland, Israel, Italy, Japan, Malaysia, Sweden,

Switzerland, Trinidad, Turkey and Uruguay.

When a meditator decides to become a teacher, he must first fulfil certain qualifications, and then he pays for the course of training required. An intending teacher needs to have been practising TM for a minimum of two years, to have completed an S.C.I. course, and to have learned the checking notes.

An S.C.I. course provides the student with an intellectual understanding of the scientific basis of TM. Studying at one's local centre at weekends, it takes about six months to complete an S.C.I. course, and consists of video tape lectures, discussions with the teacher, and set questions to be answered by the student. The questions provide a check so that the teacher, and the student himself, can see whether the student has understood the lecture properly. At the end of the course, there is an examination. Unlike a school examination, however, it is a test of understanding and not of memory. The student is allowed to consult his notes during the examination if this is found necessary but will fail the course if the answers given show that he has not understood what S.C.I. is all about.

The checking notes are what every teacher must commit to memory in order to give meditators a routine check on their meditation. It consists of a set of statements and questions to be spoken by the teacher, plus a list of possible answers to questions (mostly 'Yes' or 'no'), with instructions as to which statement relates to which answer. For example, part of the notes reads as follows:

14. Did you have some thoughts in that quietness?	'Yes'	15
15. Fine, you felt thoughts come in that quietness.	'no'	12
16. Did you notice that a thought comes effortlessly, spontaneously?	'Yes'	20
17. Alright, close the eyes again, just sit easily. (One minute)	'no'	17

The would-be teacher must learn all the phrases that are numbered (the 'reference number' for each answer to a question) and must also learn which number relates to which phrase, in any order. For the most part, the phrases which relate to a 'No' answer will not be used, and so the teacher must be able to 'jump' from one to another without hesitation. When a 'No' reply *is* given, it is often necessary to repeat the same phrase again, or to go to a much longer statement. To test the student on this, one of the teachers pretends to be a meditator who has come for a check, and the trainee must give all the correct instructions, precisely as written in the notes. If only one word is wrong, the trainee will have to spend some more time learning the notes and then take another test. Once they have been memorized, the words seem to be ingrained into the memory forever and come out as if one is speaking quite naturally. I learned the notes by first reading and re-reading them at every opportunity, and then mentally repeating them whenever I had nothing else to think about. I did not quite get it right on the first test, but by the time I had my second test I had memorized not only the necessary parts, but also all of the preamble and the exact wording of all the ancilliary instructions.

It is necessary to have final instruction from Maharishi personally and to undergo extensive periods of extra meditation. This naturally means taking an extended 'holiday' from work, in order to go to wherever the training is given, so there is the cost of travel and loss of earnings to consider. Some progress is being made towards being able to do all the training at a local centre on a part-time basis, which would obviously allow many more people to become teachers.

What has been possible for several years is to pay for the course itself by working for the movement. Assistance is always required at one or other of the main centres, doing jobs ranging from cooking to writing letters. For every three days worked, the trainee will receive one day's free tuition. Although this does not completely absorb the cost, it is a considerable help. No payment is made to the trainee for the work he does, but comfortable accommodation and food is provided free of charge.

The TM movement is often criticized for charging a fee, and quite a high one at that, for teaching a very simple procedure. The feeling is that all spiritual guidance should be free. But since TM must be taught on an individual level, there must of necessity be a network of training centres, all of which need to be staffed and paid for. There is a further point about charging a fee for TM which is worthy of consideration. Maharishi has often likened TM to a large and valuable stone found in the desert by a traveller. If the traveller picks it up thinking that it might be valuable, but not knowing quite how valuable, he will probably carry it for a while. However, if he has a long way to walk and the stone begins to feel heavy or become uncomfortable, he may just throw it away. Likewise with TM, if it is provided free and the results are not immediate, the person may stop meditating just because he cannot really be bothered to do it. However, if a fee is charged, the meditator will want to get his money's worth. If he feels that there is some cause for complaint, he will return to the centre, and there he will receive an explanation. Perhaps he is not doing it correctly, or has not given it a fair trial. At least he will want to keep trying it to see if anything happens. This is more beneficial both for the meditator himself and for the purpose of the World Plan.

Of special interest is the TM-Sidhi programme, which has recently had quite a lot of public attention, due to the claims that meditators can be taught to fly, make themselves invisible, and walk through solid walls! A leaflet about the TM-Sidhi course describes it as having been 'specially formulated by Maharishi to *greatly hasten the growth to enlightenment* and to provide greater enjoyment along the way ... The programme ... is designed to give the system a *far deeper degree of rest* than is gained during your two daily meditations.' (my italics) The TM-Sidhi programme is controversial, to say the least, but the principle on which levitation techniques (for instance) are based is simple enough, even though they involve advanced yogic practices to become effective. It is really a matter of mind body co-ordination. If this is improved as far as it can be, the body rises into the air because the mind tells it to do so.

CHAPTER SIX

HOW TO LEARN TM

> Ask, and it shall be given you; seek, and ye shall find; knock, and it shall be opened unto you.
>
> Matthew 7:7

Although this work is intended as an objective appraisal of TM, it seems logical to assume that after reading thus far, some readers at least will decide that they wish to learn the technique. Others may wish to find out more about it before coming to any decision. In either case, the best way to go about it is to attend one of the introductory lectures given each week by local TM centres. There is very little worse than deciding positively about something such as this, and not knowing what to do next, so I am including this final chapter for the benefit of such readers.

The first thing to clarify is that the introductory lectures are quite free, and absolutely no pressure is used to persuade anyone who attends a lecture to return for instructions. Indeed, the teachers do not even ask for names. The procedure is for one of the teachers to explain what is involved in learning the technique, and what benefits can be expected, and then to answer any questions that members of the audience may have. Those who do decide to learn at once can then make an appointment for any convenient weekend. In other cases, however, nothing more will be done by the teacher until the people decide for themselves that they wish to learn. It is worth re-stating, however, that is is not necessary to be convinced that TM works. All that is necessary is a willingness to try it out.

Almost all large towns have a local centre within easy reach and the telephone number may be listed under

'Transcendental Meditation' or 'Spiritual Regeneration Movement'. In case of difficulty, the national centres will provide information and the address of your nearest centre.

Without going into all the details of the procedure, which will of course be outlined by the teacher, it may be helpful to describe broadly what learning the technique actually involves.

It would be incorrect to feel that one is automatically joining the movement. Learning the technique basically involves attending the centre on three consecutive evenings. If the meditator wishes to attend the weekly meetings afterwards (which are also free), he is made welcome. If not, he is left alone and simply meditates as instructed in his own time. Certainly nobody writes or visits anyone to ask why they have not attended any meetings. It used to be common practice to send out newsletters to every address on the register, but due to the expense and the fact that many meditators move without informing the centre, the newsletters are now only sent on subscription.

During the first two years, the meditator is strongly advised to have regular checks on his procedure, which are included in the instruction fee. This only takes about half an hour, and is simply to ensure that the meditation is being performed correctly. Any complaints that the meditator may have will be dealt with at these sessions. Checking is recommended at monthly intervals for the first six months and quarterly for the next eighteen months. Even after the two year period, when the meditation is assumed to be 'established', it is useful to be checked occasionally. Also if for any reason the practice is stopped, it is wise to arrange for a check when starting again.

After the introductory lecture, the first step towards actually learning the technique is of course to complete the application form and pay the fee. Fees vary according to the status of the applicant, so no specific figures can be quoted here. For instance, full time students and unemployed persons are charged less than the standard rate, and there is a special rate for married couples. In fact during recruiting drives, and in other special circumstances, instructions may be given free or for a token donation. However, the general feeling seems to be that it is better for the initiate to make some kind of financial sacrifice, since he will then be more disposed towards giving the technique a fair trial.

Another commitment is to cease taking any unprescribed drugs for fifteen days before instruction. This is not a moral judgement about drugs, but merely to make the nervous system properly prepared for the initial experience. Cigarettes are not included in this requirement, and neither is alcohol.

For the first evening, the initiate is asked to bring a clean white handkerchief, some fruit and some flowers. These articles are used in a short ceremony, during which the teacher recites in Sanskrit. The ceremony is to remind the teacher and the pupil that they are sharing age-old knowledge.

Immediately after the ceremony, the initiate is told his mantra and instructed how to use it. Then he is taken to a spare room for his first twenty-minute meditation, during which time the teacher will probably be initiating someone else. At the end of the twenty minutes, the teacher or someone else will quietly enter the room and tell the initiate that it is time to stop. The initiate then completes a form to describe his experience during the meditation. Apart from any questions that may arise, this is the end of the first evening's instruction.

On the following evenings, the procedure is a group meditation, with all the people who have been initiated in that week meditating in a room together, under the guidance of one of the teachers. This is followed by another questionnaire and a general discussion. The teacher goes into greater detail about how to meditate, the TM movement, higher states of consciousness, and so on, and again answers any questions that arise.

By the end of the third evening, the new meditator should know enough to practise TM by himself and should also have a fair understanding of what the TM philosophy is all about. The revelations about Cosmic Consciousness, the World Plan and so on can be rather overwhelming at first, and one tends to forget other points about the technique. It is therefore worth the effort to attend at least some of the weekly 'follow-up' meetings if it is convenient, if only to remind oneself just why one is meditating.

TM is only a part of a world-wide movement – a revolution in consciousness arising out of an increasing awareness of impending disaster. To avert global catastrophe, in whatever form it threatens, requires fundamental changes in the way we view ourselves and in how we relate to other people. The practice of TM is playing a vital role in this process by raising the level of individual consciousness and thus diminishing the possibility of ego-centred aggression and selfish exploitation – of others and of the Earth itself. As Maharishi himself says:

> Although there are certainly many things in the world to be put right, we shall not be able to accomplish this humane ideal by merely shuffling the environment. It will never humanly succeed until we can see and appreciate that environment at its full value, until we can envision all its possibilities with expanded mind and heart so that they may be actualized to the advantage of everyone and everything in nature.

APPENDIX

Addresses of national centres are as follows:

Great Britain
The Spiritual Regeneration Movement of Great Britain
32 Cranbourn Street
London WC2H 7EY

U.S.A.
Students' International Meditation Society
1015 Gayley Avenue
Los Angeles
California 90024

Canada
Students' International Meditation Society
Office 2
840 Port Street
Victoria BC

Australia
Transcendental Meditation Centre
29 Drummond Street
Carlton
Melbourne
Victoria 3053

New Zealand
The Spiritual Regeneration Movement Foundation of New Zealand
17 Horoeka Avenue
Mount Eden
Auckland 3

South Africa
Spiritual Regeneration Centre
Rossiter Street
Tamboers Kloof
Cape Town

India
Spiritual Regeneration Movement Foundation of India
The Academy of Meditation
Shankaracharya Nagar
Rishikesh UP

INDEX